THE
ENCYCLOPEDIA
OF
Energy
Healing

An A-to-Z Guide *to* Spiritual Elements *and* How to Use Them

MYSTIC MICHAELA

Author of *The Angel Numbers Book*

Adams Media

New York   Amsterdam/Antwerp   London   Toronto   Sydney/Melbourne   New Delhi

Adams Media
An Imprint of Simon & Schuster, LLC
100 Technology Center Drive
Stoughton, MA 02072

First Adams Media hardcover edition June 2026

ADAMS MEDIA and colophon are registered trademarks of Simon & Schuster, LLC.

Simon & Schuster strongly believes in freedom of expression and stands against censorship in all its forms. For more information, visit BooksBelong.com.

For information about special discounts for bulk purchases, please contact Simon & Schuster Special Sales at 1-866-506-1949 or business@simonandschuster.com.

The Simon & Schuster Speakers Bureau can bring authors to your live event. For more information or to book an event, contact the Simon & Schuster Speakers Bureau at 1-866-248-3049 or visit our website at www.simonspeakers.com.

Interior design by Colleen Cunningham
Interior images © 123RF; Adobe Stock; Getty Images; iStockphoto

Manufactured in China

10 9 8 7 6 5 4 3 2 1

Library of Congress Control Number: 2025950178

ISBN 978-1-5072-2633-9
ISBN 978-1-5072-2634-6 (ebook)

Contains material adapted from the following title published by Adams Media, an Imprint of Simon & Schuster, LLC: *The Encyclopedia of Crystals, Herbs, & New Age Elements* by Adams Media, copyright © 2016, ISBN 978-1-4405-9109-9.

Contents

Introduction

Energy surrounds you: It serves as the invisible thread connecting your existence in this plane to all living things. This energy also lies within you. It fuels your body, keeping you healthy, bringing you inner peace, and fostering spiritual enlightenment. This energy requires care just like your body does, however, and if the energy within and around you is blocked, stagnant, or otherwise imbalanced, your physical and mental health can suffer. Energy healing is a practice that aims to address energy imbalances or blockages that contribute to mental and physical pain or illness, limiting life patterns, and poor spiritual conditions.

Energy healing is an effective, time-honored tradition that can transform how you think and feel. In fact, for thousands of years, stones, herbs, and other natural elements have been used in cultures around the world to restore energy—thereby promoting health and prosperity, providing spiritual protection, easing pain and suffering, and inspiring spiritual growth. Today, energy healing can work hand in hand with modern advances to support holistic health.

The Encyclopedia of Energy Healing is a comprehensive compilation of that powerful shared wisdom, highly valued and passed down for generations, for the ultimate purpose of healing yourself and others. Whether you're new to energy healing or have been practicing it for years, this guidebook will lead you on the path toward emotional and spiritual health by way of natural resources. In it, you'll find crystals, flowers, and essential oils alongside timeless techniques like sipping teas, burning herbs, and practicing yoga, as well as modern options like EFT tapping. For example, you can:

- Hold a piece of amber while meditating to tap into the wisdom of your ancestors.
- Burn fennel as incense to purify a space.

- Diffuse tea tree oil to boost energy levels and build self-confidence.
- Use a singing bowl to clear negativity, balance chakras, and relieve stress.
- Try hypnosis to deepen your connection with a higher consciousness and reroute negative behavior patterns.

Each chapter focuses on a different energy healing practice and helps you appreciate its history and integrate its power into your own life. From spiritual protection to physical healing to personal growth, these traditions can transform your overall well-being. When you give your energy care and attention, you will feel restored, resilient, and more in touch with your inner self.

Your energy is the core of who you are, and the foundation of life on planet Earth. Empower yourself to strengthen your spiritual connection, improve your health, and harness your inner light with *The Encyclopedia of Energy Healing*.

Getting Started in Energy Healing

Energy healing encompasses a wide range of practices. Some of the items here—such as herbs, spices, and essential oils—will likely be familiar, as you may already have them in your spice cabinet, garden, or backyard. If so, you'll gain a deeper understanding of these resources and learn additional ways to use them. Other ideas, like astral projection, color therapy, and labyrinth walking, may be new to you, but you'll find simple ways to incorporate them into your energy healing practice.

In this brief section, you'll learn foundational information about energy healing that will help you fully engage with the elements described in this book. You'll also find an explanation of how the book is set up and ideas for how to choose which elements are best suited for your path to energy healing.

Embracing Holistic Medicine

Many of the remedies and practices in this book belong to the tradition of holistic healing, a diverse field of alternative medicine that treats the whole person, not just a single ailment or condition. Practitioners of holistic medicine believe that a person is made up of parts and if one part isn't working properly, it has a negative effect on the whole. Holistic healthcare practices covered in this book include herbal medicine, acupuncture, and massage.

Understanding Chakras

Throughout the book, you will engage with your own personal energy centers: chakras. In Hindu, yogic, and other traditions, seven chakras are spiritual centers of the body, arranged vertically along the spine. When you open yourself to the wisdom of your chakras, you welcome a new level of consciousness that can help you balance your energy and tend to ailments.

Each chakra governs a different kind of energy and connects to an area of the physical body.

The seven major chakras are:

- **Crown chakra:** Located at the top of the head, the crown chakra controls mental energy and is our connection to the divine.
- **Third eye chakra:** This chakra, located between the eyes, is the seat of intuition. It governs imagination, wisdom, and decision-making.
- **Throat chakra:** The throat chakra rules communication and expression, and is the source of personal truth.
- **Heart chakra:** This chakra is found in the middle of the chest and is all about love, joy, and inner peace.
- **Solar plexus or navel chakra:** This is the power chakra, the core self, located in the center of the abdomen.
- **Sacral or base chakra:** This is the pleasure center of the body, located in the lower abdomen, below the navel. It is the source of confidence and self-worth, and it also rules sexuality.
- **Root chakra:** Located at the base of the spine, this chakra is the foundation of the body and governs spiritual and physical grounding.

How to Use This Book

The Encyclopedia of Energy Healing gathers some of the most profound and transformative elements and practices of energy healing: stones, herbs, flowers, scent, fire and light, sound, insight, symbols, movement, and touch. Each entry offers:

- A Description section, which outlines basic details and honors the historical background and geographical significance of the practice.
- A History and Lore section, which gives you insight into how the element was used in ancient healing practices and rituals.
- A Uses section, which suggests modern ways to weave these healing practices into your life. Activities such as meditating, chanting, and Reiki can awaken you to a new level of well-being and fulfillment.

You can read this book from beginning to end or use the table of contents or the index to quickly find practices that align with your physical and spiritual needs. Be sure to check the glossary to discover any unfamiliar terms you encounter along the way.

Invite this encyclopedia to be your guide on your journey through energy healing. The path you are embarking upon links you to thousands of years of others who also sought healing, protection, and spiritual connection. While your experience will be personal to you, allow yourself to feel the immeasurable power of a goal shared across the planes of time—one of health, healing, and connection with nature.

1

The Power of Crystals and Gemstones

Crystals, stones, and gemstones have fascinated humans across cultures and throughout time. Gazing at a striking clear quartz in the light or beholding the stunning hue of an amethyst, it's easy to get lost in their mysterious power. Stones have been used for millennia to treat physical ailments and balance the energies of the body, as well as to foster mental, emotional, and spiritual well-being.

There are many ways to incorporate these stones on your path to energetic wellness. In certain traditions, stones or crystals are placed directly on the body to heal physical pain or energy misalignment. They can also be placed nearby as you conduct rituals to restore energy fields, cleanse the aura, and promote a peaceful space. Wearing certain gemstones while setting strong intentions can amplify their power.

These stones work through their energetic resonance and vibration, and their connection to our planet. Many contain additional minerals and other substances that harness the power of the earth to heal your body and mind. For example, the high concentration of copper in malachite can help reduce the swelling and inflammation that cause joint and muscle pain, and an analgesic called succinic acid is released when amber is warmed by the skin, making it helpful for addressing arthritis and toothaches.

Stones can be found in one of two forms: (1) raw or (2) tumbled or polished. Both forms are effective, but they should be cared for in different ways. Raw stones are in their natural state, which means they may be sharp-edged or craggy and can be fragile. Tumbled or polished stones have been "tumbled" with fine sand or grit to smooth their edges. As a result of this process, tumbled stones are much more durable than raw stones and can be kept together (in a soft bag, for example), whereas raw stones should be kept separate to prevent scratching and breakage. You choose which type aligns with your physical and spiritual needs.

There are also two main approaches to choosing a crystal or gemstone: You may be looking to treat a specific ailment or issue, or you may be simply searching for a stone that resonates with you. If you are completely new to the world of stones, your birthstone might be a meaningful place to start. Otherwise, you can choose a stone by visiting a local store and browsing through its offerings. If a stone catches your eye, pick it up, hold it in your hand, and see how it feels. Trust your intuition. A stone that attracts your attention and feels right is the stone for you.

Agate

Description

Agate is a form of chalcedony, which is a variety of quartz. Agates form in cavities in volcanic rock. Water and carbon dioxide bubble out of the volcanic rock and rise to the surface, and over time the minerals crystalize in layers. This is why agates generally have a banded appearance, with layers of different colors. Agate is found all over the world, but was named for the Achates River (now the Dirillo River) on the island of Sicily, Italy, where it was first discovered.

History and Lore

The use of agate goes back to the Neolithic era (or the New Stone Age), when it was popular for both healing and decoration. The ancient Greeks had many uses for agate. For example, moss agate, which doesn't have the classic layered appearance of agate but instead has colors and patterns that resemble plant life or landscapes, was considered helpful in ensuring a plentiful harvest. Many cultures throughout history have believed that wearing agate protects against tragedy and evil.

Uses

Healing Uses

There are many varieties of agate, and each kind has its own healing uses. Wearing agate near affected areas of the body either as an adornment or during meditation can alleviate specific conditions. For example, blue lace agate, named for its lavender-blue color and lace-like pattern, is a calming stone that is thought to soothe headaches, digestive discomfort, and skin issues (especially eczema) when worn near the affected areas of the body. Fire agate, whose iridescent rainbow colors resemble a flame, can increase circulation, battle lethargy, and improve mood. Because of agate's connection with the throat chakra, it is often worn around the neck to soothe coughs, sore throats, and even dental issues.

Personal Protection

Agates exhibit both the strength of a stone and the fluidity of air and water, making them useful as balancing and grounding stones. As they transmute emotions, they're excellent for stabilizing energy and combating negativity and bitterness. Agates are often used in ceremonies concerning love, healing, protection, and courage, and it is believed that a person can't tell a lie when looking at an agate.

Spatial Protection

Because agates can protect from negative energies and allow calming vibrations to flow freely, place them in any area of your home that would benefit from a gentle, calming influence. For example, they can be positioned at entry points and in living areas to welcome calm energy and promote respectful conversation. Different varieties of agate can be used for different purposes. A blue lace agate can be helpful in a home gym or office to encourage health and prosperity, while a fire agate can be placed in the bedroom to support passion and romance.

Personal/Spiritual Growth

You may wish to use a slice of agate as a coaster under your morning coffee to assist with centering yourself before the day ahead, or hold a stone during meditation to quiet the mind. Agates help raise self-awareness and consciousness, encouraging reflection that can lead to deep spiritual understanding and growth. Known to heighten focus, they can also enhance mental function and improve concentration and analytical thinking, which can be helpful for problem-solving. Additionally, agates can be used to boost confidence and are particularly helpful with public speaking and other communication-related challenges.

Amber

Description

Contrary to its appearance, amber is neither a stone nor a crystal—it's actually fossilized tree resin. Trees secrete resin to heal wounds and protect themselves against disease, and over time the resin dries and hardens. Long after the tree is gone, the resin remains, and over the course of millions of years it becomes amber. Amber deposits have been found in places all over the world, including Mexico, the Dominican Republic, and the coast of the Baltic Sea. Baltic amber is the most well-known variety.

History and Lore

Amber has long been used in jewelry and other types of ornamentation, and many cultures have believed it holds magical powers. The ancient Greeks used amber to promote good health and ward off evil. The Aztecs and the Maya burned it as incense. Today, in addition to its continued use in jewelry and other art objects, amber is also valuable in the field of science for the insects and plant life it often contains.

Uses

Healing Uses

Amber contains an analgesic called succinic acid, which is released when it is warmed by the skin. For this reason, necklaces and bracelets of amber beads are worn to ease arthritis and joint pain. Amber is an ingredient in many ointments and creams for burns and insect bites, and it is also used in cosmetics to destroy free radicals associated with aging. Wearing amber on a very long chain opens the solar plexus chakra (which is near the belly button), strengthening your personal power and confidence.

Personal Protection

Amber can be used for psychic or physical protection and is a great tool for grounding your aura. Because amber is warm to the touch and yellow or orange in color, many believe it holds the power of the sun, which was absorbed by the ancient trees that produced it. Holding amber in meditation is thought to assist in tapping into the wisdom of ancestors and remembering past lives, and also to improve memory. Bring one in your pocket during examinations to assist with recall. Amber is also considered a karmic stone, or a stone that resolves unfavorable patterns not only of your present life, but of past lives as well. It is thought to invite positive energy and bring balance to disruptive and chaotic forces around you. Placing it in your home creates an energy of stability and clarity, and amber has long been used as a shield against unwanted spiritual energies.

Spatial Protection

Placing a piece of amber in the living room or main gathering place of your home is thought to create a feeling of balance and calm. Due to amber's absorption of ancient knowledge, putting it in office spaces or a reading nook encourages self-exploration and wisdom. Displaying amber in spaces where family gathers strengthens relationships, since it is thought to assist in emotional stability.

Personal/Spiritual Growth

Amber helps you connect to your inner wisdom, bridging the gap between your everyday self and your spiritual core. Because it can open your solar plexus chakra, it brings out your innate talents and abilities and enhances creativity so that you may more easily achieve your goals.

Amethyst

Description

Amethyst is a variety of crystalline quartz that ranges in color from violet to mauve. The color of the amethyst changes in response to heat; depending on the temperature, it can become a range of colors, from reddish brown to yellow and even colorless. The majority of the world's commercial citrine is actually heat-treated amethyst (see Citrine entry in this chapter). The most significant deposits of amethyst are found in southern Brazil, Uruguay, and Madagascar, and it is also found in parts of Germany and Russia.

History and Lore

According to legend, the Greek god of wine, Dionysus, once pursued a nymph named Amethyst, who wished to escape his advances. The nymph asked for the help of the goddess Diana, who transformed her into a clear crystal. When Dionysus saw what she had done, he angrily threw wine on the crystal, giving it its purple color. The ancient Egyptians believed amethyst could assuage fear and guilt, and the Greeks and Romans used it to help avoid overindulgence in food and alcohol.

Uses

Healing Uses

Amethyst is known for its stress-reducing attributes, and its ability to quell overactive thoughts. It can also strengthen the immune system and increase feelings of happiness and self-love. For headaches, rub an amethyst crystal on your forehead. Since it's regarded for its sleep benefits, placing amethyst under your pillow combats insomnia, brings pleasant dreams, and assists in dream recall.

Personal Protection

This purple crystal has calming effects, defending against stress and negative energy. Amethyst is connected to the third eye chakra (located between the eyes), which is responsible for intuition, and the crown chakra (at the top of the head), which represents a connection to spiritual energy. Wear amethyst jewelry to heighten intuitive awareness and relieve tension. In conflict situations, holding amethyst brings feelings of serenity.

Spatial Protection

Amethyst is a protective stone that repels negative energy and supports tranquility. Placing it in your bedroom offers respite from racing thoughts, which can interfere with sleep, and bathing with the stone removes the stress and energetic buildup of the day. (You can either place these crystals on the edge of your tub or fully submerge them in the water.)

Personal/Spiritual Growth

Amethyst is the birthstone for the month of February. It facilitates spiritual awareness, energizes depleted energy, and forges a connection to the inner self. It also protects against psychic danger and the results of energetic exhaustion, especially during spiritual exploration. Amethyst is a great choice to hold during meditation practices because it helps ease the transition to a meditative state and encourages focus.

Aquamarine

Description

Aquamarine is a blue-green, transparent variety of the mineral beryl, which is colorless in its pure form. The blue-green color of aquamarine is a result of the presence of iron in the crystal. The word *aquamarine* comes from the Latin *aqua marina*, meaning "seawater." The stone is quite common, with major deposits occurring in Brazil, and it has also been found in other parts of the world, including the United States.

History and Lore

Greek sailors believed aquamarine was the treasure of mermaids, and carried it for good luck and protection as well as to prevent seasickness on sea voyages. The crystal was believed to be especially powerful when immersed in water. The Romans used aquamarine to cure throat, liver, and stomach ailments. Aquamarine has long been used to counteract the forces of evil and win the favor of the spirits.

Uses

Healing Uses

This crystal strengthens the cleansing organs of the body, as it is thought to detoxify the liver, spleen, and kidneys. It is also associated with the throat and heart chakras. For this reason, wearing an aquamarine necklace can help regulate thyroid issues. Working with aquamarine in meditation can calm an overactive immune system and is therefore helpful with allergies. It is also useful to combat inflammation.

Personal Protection

Aquamarine is a calming and clarifying stone that is helpful for filtering out unwanted thoughts, clearing up confusion, and bringing closure. With the tranquilizing energy of the sea, aquamarine is ruled by the moon. To recharge and cleanse an aquamarine crystal, place it in water on the night of a full moon. Carry this stone on boat or plane trips over water, as it is thought to protect sea voyagers.

Spatial Protection

Aquamarine uses water energy, which is characterized by stillness, quiet strength, and purification. Placing this crystal in spaces where there is an abundance of interpersonal interaction will assist in the maintenance of decorum and navigation of any tricky social situations. Carrying this stone in your pocket while having difficult conversations with others provides support with compassion and reduces judgmental behavior.

Personal/Spiritual Growth

Aquamarine is the birthstone for the month of March. Like water itself, it is known for providing reflective assistance with shadow work. Aquamarine also accelerates determination and reason, and therefore is helpful for focusing energy toward the accomplishment of goals. When meditating with aquamarine, imagine yourself standing before a pool of clear, blue water. Release any negative emotions into the water and watch them float away.

Aventurine

Description

Aventurine is a variety of quartz with inclusions of mica and other minerals that give it a sparkling appearance. The stone can be opaque or semi-translucent and is commonly green in color; other colors include blue, brown, and peach. Its name comes from the Italian phrase *a ventura*, meaning "by chance," pertaining to either its discovery or the randomness of the inclusions found in the stone. Deposits are found in Brazil, Austria, Russia, India, and Tanzania.

History and Lore

Some ancient Asian cultures prized aventurine and often used it for the eyes of statues, believing it improved sight and creativity. In many cultures, aventurine is considered an opportunity stone that brings good luck in any situation, from a first date to a job interview. It is often referred to as the "gambler's stone" and is especially associated with money and games of chance. Many also believe that aventurine can guard against environmental and electromagnetic pollution.

Uses

Healing Uses

Green is the color of healing, and green aventurine is considered an all-purpose healing stone. Specifically, it is associated with eyesight and is therefore helpful to people with near- or far-sightedness or astigmatism. It is also associated with the heart chakra, making it an excellent stone for people with cardiac or circulatory problems. Wearing a necklace with an aventurine pendant places the stone near the heart and increases its benefits.

Personal Protection

Aventurine is a very positive stone. Its natural calming attributes work to dissolve stress, anger, and anxiety, and produce an overall sense of harmony and calm. Aventurine is especially useful when enduring disappointment or heartbreak, as it introduces a feeling of lightness and an understanding that everything in life is temporary. It is thought to be a lucky stone, and when carried, is able to attract opportunities for love and financial abundance.

Spatial Protection

Placing aventurine in the social places of a home, such as the living room or kitchen, encourages harmonious emotional connections and interactions. Decorating your home garden with aventurine stones is thought to promote plant growth and vitality. Displaying this crystal on windowsills and in doorways is believed to bring positive energy into your home.

Personal/Spiritual Growth

Also known as "the stone of opportunity," aventurine has a stabilizing effect on the mind and encourages perseverance in difficult times. It is helpful in letting go of old habits and disappointments and allowing you to move into the future. The stone encourages optimism and increases motivation, helping you to achieve your goals. Meditating with aventurine can be helpful during times that feel stagnant.

Calcite

Description

Calcite is the most common form of calcium carbonate, the major mineral in limestone, marble, and chalk. It is colorless or white in its pure form, but can be almost any color—pink, red, orange, yellow, green, blue, brown, black, or gray—when impurities are present. Calcite is very soft (a 3 on the Mohs scale, which measures a stone's hardness) and can be easily scratched, so it is rarely used in jewelry. However, it is frequently used as a component within construction materials such as cement, mortar, floor tiles, and countertops, as well as in paints and fertilizers. The clearest form of calcite is called Iceland spar, because it is common in Iceland. Calcite is also found in England, Italy, Germany, Romania, Mexico, and the United States.

History and Lore

Calcite gets its name from the Latin *calx*, meaning "lime." The ancient Egyptians favored it as an artisan material because of its softness and workability, and they used a harder, banded variety of calcite called alabaster to make ornamental and ceremonial objects such as sculptures and cosmetic containers. Calcite has often been referred to as a "stone of the mind" and is believed to improve cognitive function.

Uses

Healing Uses

Due to its acid-neutralizing effects, calcium carbonate is the major active ingredient in most commercially available antacid tablets, such as Rolaids and TUMS. Calcite crystals can be used to encourage calcium absorption or to dissolve areas of calcification in the body, making them useful for strengthening bones. Green calcite is preferred for heart-centered healing, blue for calming the nervous system, and orange for boosting your creativity.

Personal Protection

Carrying this stone, or handling it carefully in jewelry, allows for easier access to its beneficial properties. Pink calcite is powerful for releasing fear and grief and clearing a path for forgiveness. Blue calcite is a soothing stone that aids in recuperation and relaxation. It is also associated with the throat chakra and therefore aids in communication. Black calcite can strengthen past-life regression sessions and recalling memories with the goal of letting go of the past. It also helps alleviate depression and stress following a traumatic experience.

Spatial Protection

This is a great stone to have anywhere in your home, as it removes negative energies from the environment around it. In particular, calcite clears stagnant energies and is ideal for a home office or a workspace, as it supports an uplifting vibration. Not only is it considered a booster for productivity; it assists with promoting harmonious interactions between coworkers. Its translucence also makes for eye-catching decor as a polished slab or carving.

Personal/Spiritual Growth

Calcite is a powerful energy cleanser and a stabilizing stone. It can be used to calm the mind, connect with the intellect, and boost emotional intelligence. It also enhances learning abilities, making it a wonderful stone for students to have nearby as they work. Red calcite removes emotional barriers that prevent forward movement in life. Yellow or golden calcite is helpful to hold during meditation, as it encourages a deep state of relaxation and opens the mind to spiritual guidance.

Carnelian

Description

Carnelian is a variety of chalcedony that ranges in color from pink to reddish orange to brownish red. The color is a result of iron impurities in the crystal. Natural carnelian is increasingly rare, and many of the carnelian crystals on the market are actually agates that have been dyed and heat-treated. Agates masquerading as carnelian stones will have a striped appearance when held up to the light, while natural carnelian will have a more consistent, cloudy appearance. It's often used in jewelry, such as cameos and intaglios (images carved into a stone, such as carnelian intaglio rings). The most significant source of carnelian is India, but it is also found in the United States, Peru, Brazil, Uruguay, and Madagascar.

History and Lore

The name *carnelian* derives from the Latin word *carneus*, meaning "flesh." The ancient Egyptians considered carnelian sacred—linked to the goddess Isis—and thought that it possessed feminine energy. The ancient Greeks and Romans wore it to protect against sin. The prophet Muhammad is said to have worn a silver ring with an engraved carnelian stone on the little finger of his right hand, making it an important stone for Muslims. The emperor Napoleon famously wore an octagonal carnelian ring that he found in the sands of Egypt.

Uses

Healing Uses

Due its vibrant energy as well as its red color and iron content, this stone is associated with blood and vitality; it can be used to cleanse the blood, stanch excessive blood flow, and heal open wounds. It also is believed to increase fertility and is believed beneficial if kept nearby during childbirth. Wearing carnelian stones closer to the lower chakras may improve vitamin and mineral absorption, and help ensure healthy circulation. Carnelian connects with the sacral chakra, located between the navel and the pubic bone, which rules creativity.

Personal Protection

Carnelian is often used to protect against physical harm and accidents. It is a great stone to use in past-life regressions or in the search for a "twin soul" or family. Its association with the element of fire makes it helpful for rekindling passion or romance. Carnelian can also be used to cleanse other stones.

Spatial Protection

Carnelian uses fire energy, bringing warmth, illumination, and passion to a space. Keep carnelian near the front door of your home to secure protection from thieves and unwanted visitors. In a workspace, it is thought to welcome abundance and protect against bad word of mouth against a business.

Personal/Spiritual Growth

This stone promotes peace and protects against negative emotions, both internal and external. It grounds its owner in the present reality and encourages acceptance while banishing envy, rage, and resentment. Carnelian assists with decision-making and clarity as it combats stagnation and provides energy. Keep it on your person if you're looking for motivation and a creativity boost.

Chalcedony

Description

Chalcedony is a microcrystalline type of quartz and belongs to a broad category that includes some of the other stones in this chapter, such as agate, carnelian, and onyx. "True" or "actual" chalcedony is milky white, gray, or blue, and often has a glowing, translucent quality. The stone is found all over the world, including the United States, Mexico, Brazil, Uruguay, India, and Madagascar. The name *chalcedony* is most likely derived from *Chalcedon*, the name of an ancient Greek city in Asia Minor.

History and Lore

Chalcedony has been in use since the Bronze Age, when it was favored for carving seals, intaglios, and rings and other jewelry. The Roman orator Cicero is said to have worn a blue chalcedony stone around his neck due to its reputation for being beneficial during public speaking. Native Americans believed chalcedony to be sacred and used it in spiritual ceremonies.

Uses

Healing Uses

You may place the stone on your throat in meditation or wear it as jewelry for a more consistent presence. Chalcedony promotes healing by boosting the immune system. It assists in mineral absorption and prevents mineral buildup in the body, and it can also be used to support lactation in breastfeeding mothers. Additionally, chalcedony is said to lessen the effects of dementia and Alzheimer's. Blue chalcedony is associated with the throat chakra, making it effective for soothing sore throats and other ailments of the neck area.

Personal Protection

Chalcedony is a nurturing stone often used to inspire goodwill and stabilize relationships, as well as to assist in telepathy and thought transmission. It absorbs and dissipates negative energy, paving the way for openness, generosity, and joy. You could wear chalcedony for protection while traveling or to prevent bad dreams. Working with blue chalcedony is thought to lessen the effect of illnesses associated with changes in the weather.

Spatial Protection

Blue chalcedony is thought to calm, purify, and strengthen a communal space, especially one used for reflection or prayer. Pink chalcedony is believed to foster kindness and compassion, and is helpful in bathrooms or bedrooms.

Personal/Spiritual Growth

Chalcedony is often called the "speaker's stone," as it can ease self-doubt and facilitate clear communication. It is especially helpful to actors, singers, salespeople, and others whose voices play a central role in their lives or careers. To ease public speaking jitters, hold or wear this stone while presenting. Placing a piece of white chalcedony somewhere you tend to glance at often, such as near a clock, will enhance your spiritual connection. Blue chalcedony is a creative stone that opens the mind to new ideas, enhances listening skills, and improves memory.

Citrine

Description

Citrine is a variety of crystalline quartz that ranges in color from pale yellow to reddish brown, depending on its origin and whether it is natural or heat-treated. Due to its color, it is often mistakenly referred to as gold topaz. Natural citrine, found in Spain, France, Russia, Madagascar, and the Democratic Republic of the Congo, is quite rare. Most commercial citrine is actually heat-treated amethyst, much of which comes from Brazil.

History and Lore

Citrine has been in use for thousands of years. The name derives from the French word *citron*, meaning "lemon." It was used as a decorative gem during the Hellenistic period in ancient Greece, and some biblical scholars believe citrine is the tenth of twelve stones in Aaron's breastplate in the Book of Exodus. Citrine jewelry was very popular during the Victorian and Art Deco eras, when it was commonly used in pendants and brooches. Often called the "merchant's stone," it is thought to assist in the acquisition and maintenance of wealth.

Uses

Healing Uses

This crystal aids in digestion, stimulates circulation, and regulates the metabolism. It can also address depression, anger, and mood swings. Citrine is helpful in removing toxins, especially from food or chemical exposures. Wear citrine in contact with the skin of the fingers or the throat for best results.

Personal Protection

Citrine is a success and prosperity crystal. It combats negative energy and paves the way for growth. Use citrine to manifest abundance, both physically and spiritually. Place citrine in the center of a crystal grid, carry a citrine crystal in your wallet or purse to attract money or curb overspending, or incorporate citrine while meditating on your goals to achieve abundance in the broader sense. Citrine can also be used as an "aura protector," warning against oncoming threats.

Spatial Protection

Placing citrine in the financial area of your home or business, such as in the cash box or recordkeeping book, supports abundance. Slipping it under your pillow is thought to benefit your sleep and emotional balance.

Personal/Spiritual Growth

Along with topaz, citrine is the birthstone for the month of November. Wearing citrine raises self-esteem and combats destructive tendencies. It is specifically associated with the solar plexus chakra, which is the power chakra and the core self. Wearing a long necklace with a citrine pendant will stimulate this chakra (located in the abdomen between the rib cage and the navel) and encourage creativity. Meditating with citrine facilitates access to inner thought.

Clear Quartz

Description

Clear quartz, also called rock crystal, is a hard mineral composed of silicon dioxide, which is present in a variety of rocks, including sandstone and granite. It is the second most abundant mineral on earth after feldspar and is located all over the world. Its abundance is attributed to its stability at a wide range of pressures and temperatures within the earth and its resistance to physical weathering once it has surfaced. The origin of the word *quartz* is unknown (although it may come from the Slavic word for "hard"), but the word *crystal* comes from the Greek word *krustallos*, meaning "ice." Clear quartz crystal comes in many forms, including tumbled stones, pillars or points, and clusters. Natural clear quartz should not be confused with lead crystal, such as Swarovski, which is man-made.

History and Lore

According to an ancient Japanese creation myth, quartz formed from the breath of the revered white dragon and was believed to represent perfection. Aboriginal Australians used quartz in their rain and cleansing rituals. Crystal balls made of clear quartz have been used to divine the future since the Middle Ages, possibly earlier.

Uses

Healing Uses

Clear quartz is an all-purpose healing stone often referred to as a "master healer" because it is believed to amplify healing energy. Quartz crystals can be used for any condition, but they are especially effective for stimulating the immune system and cleansing the organs. Placing quartz crystals on the body during meditation clears blockages. Acupuncture needles coated in quartz are said to increase the effectiveness of the procedure.

Personal Protection

Quartz crystals are protective shields, and wearing them as jewelry is thought to repel unwanted spiritual influences and purify your personal space. This crystal also creates a barrier against electromagnetic pollution, and wearing it filters out unwanted energies from the multitude of devices you interact with daily. You can submerge clear quartz in bathwater to remove negative energy from the body.

Spatial Protection

Due to its heightened energetic vibrations, a clear quartz cluster placed near your bed is not a good idea, as it can bring too much energy to the space and prevent restful sleep. Instead, place it where you journal and create intentions to bring focus and positivity to your thoughts. Quartz is also thought to purify the air, making it a beneficial crystal to hang anywhere in your living space.

Personal/Spiritual Growth

Quartz crystals typically have six facets, which represent the six chakras from the root to the third eye, with the point of the crystal representing the crown chakra (top of the head). This crystal works to increase consciousness, aids in past-life recall, and attracts love. Clear quartz is both colorless and contains every color of the rainbow, and therefore works on all levels of being. It removes negative energy and promotes clarity of thought. Use clear quartz during meditation to filter out distractions, and focus an intention upon it to allow the crystal's attributes to assist in its actualization. Wearing or carrying clear quartz, especially near the crown chakra, opens the mind to the wisdom of the spirit realm.

Diamond

Description

Diamond is a crystalline form of carbon that is usually colorless but can also be yellow, blue, brown, or pink. It is the hardest of the gemstones, rating a 10 on the Mohs scale, but is not nearly as rare as the jewelry industry suggests. Diamonds are found in many parts of the world, including Africa, Australia, Brazil, Canada, India, Russia, and the United States. The word *diamond* comes from the Greek *adamas*, meaning "hard" or "unconquerable," which also evolved into the word *adamant*.

History and Lore

Diamond was first mined in India as early as the fourth century B.C.E., and the stone eventually made its way to European markets. By the 1400s, members of Europe's elite were donning diamond accessories. The diamond was recognized as a healing stone as early as 5,000 years ago. In ancient India, healers used diamonds to strengthen the heart and brain. The ancient Greeks thought that by wearing diamonds, a warrior would become fearless in battle, and in ancient Rome, diamonds were considered wards against poison. Ancient Egyptians wore diamonds to connect themselves to the gods, and in China and Persia, diamonds were associated with good luck. According to German lore, sucking on a diamond would even stave off hunger when fasting.

Uses

Healing Uses

Diamond is known for its purification properties and is used to detoxify, balance metabolism, and aid in the relief of allergies and chronic conditions. To activate its power most effectively, place a rough diamond (not worn as jewelry) in a gallon of water and let it sit for eight hours before pouring the water into your daily bath. It is also beneficial for eye-related conditions, especially glaucoma, as well as dizziness and vertigo. Many use diamond to improve the function of the brain, nerves, and sensory organs, or to combat aging and boost energy levels.

Personal Protection

Diamond is one of the few crystals that never needs to be recharged; instead, it can be used as a support stone, amplifying the powers of other minerals. Wearing this stone creates a soothing and protective energy field around the individual, and diamond is particularly renowned for its ability to strengthen personal relationships.

Spatial Protection

Diamond is an ideal prism, both colorless and containing all the colors of the rainbow. Hang a diamond crystal in any window of your home to harness the sun's power and disperse light and energy freely throughout the space. Placing a diamond in water fountains in and around your home will help to clear negativity.

Personal/Spiritual Growth

Diamond is the birthstone for the month of April. This stone clears fear and pain and encourages fortitude, making it a special stone to have nearby while you set intentions. It is especially useful for creative individuals, as it stimulates the imagination and inspires inventiveness. Diamond also cleanses and stimulates the crown chakra, which is the connection to the divine. Soaking a rough diamond (not used for jewelry) in a glass of water for ten minutes, removing it, and then drinking the water with intention may clear any debris from around your inner light, allowing it to shine outward.

Emerald

Description

Emerald is a variety of beryl that owes its green color to the presence of the metallic element chromium and sometimes vanadium. The color ranges from light to dark green, and it can be either transparent or opaque. It is a relatively hard stone (7.5–8 on the Mohs scale), but inclusions can affect its durability. Emerald deposits have been found in Brazil, Columbia, Egypt, India, and the United States.

History and Lore

Emeralds were first mined in Egypt as early as 330 B.C.E., and the ancient Egyptian ruler Cleopatra famously loved the stone. The Incas and Aztecs of South America considered emerald to be a holy stone, but when the Spanish conquistadors arrived in the sixteenth century, they exploited those deposits for trading. One of the largest and most famous emeralds is the Mogul Emerald, measuring 217.80 carats and about 10 centimeters high. Dating from 1695, this stone is inscribed with Islamic prayers on one side and engraved with flowers on the other. In 2001, it was auctioned off at Christie's of London to an anonymous buyer for $2.2 million.

Uses

Healing Uses

Emerald stimulates the heart chakra and has a healing effect on both the emotions and the physical heart. Believed to possess a rejuvenating quality, it is also beneficial for the eyes, lungs, spine, and muscles. Worn around the neck, emerald can ease the effects of epilepsy and seizures. Emerald also aids in recovery from infectious disease. Submerging an emerald in water while bathing is another way to utilize its healing power.

Personal Protection

Emerald enhances loyalty, unity, and unconditional love, but if the stone changes color, it is a sign of unfaithfulness. Wear this stone when needed to ward off negativity and encourage positive actions, but do not wear it constantly, as this can trigger negative emotions.

Spatial Protection

Emerald encourages growth and vitality, making it helpful to place in spaces where family and friends come to eat. For this same reason, putting it in the room where small children play or sleep can be beneficial. Its connection to love and passion are why emeralds make excellent additions to a marital bedroom.

Personal/Spiritual Growth

Emerald is the birthstone for the month of May. Working through the heart chakra, this stone balances the emotions, strengthens the connection to the divine, and provides support on your spiritual journey. It is a stone of hope, allowing you to experience abundance in ways other than wealth. Emerald is especially helpful for enhancing psychic abilities and clairvoyance. That's why it is excellent to have with you during meditation, as it focuses intention, raises consciousness, and gathers wisdom—for best results, use a clear and not an opaque variety of the stone.

Fluorite

Description

Fluorite, also called fluorspar, is a mineral composed chiefly of calcium fluoride that is often fluorescent under ultraviolet light and can be a variety of colors, including blue, green, purple, yellow, and brown, as well as colorless. The word *fluorite* derives from the Latin verb *fluere*, meaning "to flow"—a reference to the stone's low melting point. It is quite common worldwide, with deposits found in Canada, the United States, Mexico, England, Germany, and China, among other locations.

History and Lore

Fluorite has long been used as what's called a flux to lower the melting point of raw materials in the production of steel and, more recently, aluminum. The phenomenon of fluorescence, first described by the mathematician and physicist George Gabriel Stokes in 1852, takes its name from fluorite. The stone's relative softness (4 on the Mohs scale) has made it popular for carving for thousands of years.

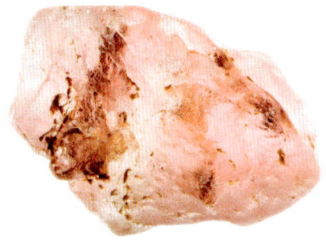

Uses

Healing Uses

Fluorite is a powerful healing stone. It is thought to promote the flow of the body's immune system. Because of this, it's often regarded as helpful for osteoporosis and may relieve pain associated with arthritis. Rubbing a fluorite crystal across the body toward the heart provides pain relief. Use fluorite in meditation or carried on the body in the form of jewelry to battle infections, viruses, and skin issues. Blue fluorite is especially helpful for ear, nose, and throat problems, while yellow fluorite releases toxins, aids the liver, and benefits cholesterol levels. Rainbow fluorite is especially helpful for energy alignment.

Personal Protection

Fluorite cleanses the aura and the chakras, especially the throat and crown chakras. This stone also has powerful protective qualities, especially on the psychic level. Use it to distinguish true feelings from outside influence as it assists with clarity.

Spatial Protection

Fluorite is known for its ability to neutralize energy. Placing fluorite towers around the home or office allows this crystal to absorb negativity from all angles and transform it to a neutral and calm vibration. At home, surround family photographs with green fluorite stones to mend broken relationships. You may also place fluorite near your computer to clear electromagnetic stress.

Personal/Spiritual Growth

Often referred to as the "genius stone," fluorite integrates spiritual energies, maximizes focus, and heightens intuitive powers. Use it in meditation to focus the mind and open the door to the subconscious. Students especially will benefit from this stone, as it enhances learning capabilities and concentration.

Garnet

Description

The term *garnet* encompasses a broad group of minerals that includes almandine (deep violet-red), andradite (green to brown or black), grossularite (pale green, pink, brown, or black), hessonite (brown or yellowish brown), melanite (black), pyrope (deep red), rhodolite (rose-red or pink), spessartite (orange and red to brownish red), and uvarovite (green). Garnet is a relatively hard stone (6.5–7.5 on the Mohs scale) and is found worldwide. The word *garnet* most likely comes from the Latin *granatum*, meaning "pomegranate."

History and Lore

Ancient Egyptian pharaohs wore red garnet necklaces in life and were entombed with them for the afterlife. The Romans wore signet rings of carved garnet and used them to stamp wax seals on important documents. Some people believe that garnet was the only source of light on Noah's ark.

Uses

Healing Uses

Garnet is a regenerative healing stone, and thought to amplify love, energy, and protection. It is believed to purify and energize the blood, heart, and lungs, as well as assist in the absorption of vitamins and minerals. Carrying this stone with you or wearing it as jewelry allows it to stimulate all chakras, from crown to root. Almandine in particular is helpful for absorbing iron. Grossularite can enhance fertility. Melanite can strengthen bones and soothe arthritis pain. Spessartite can be used to ease lactose intolerance and address calcium imbalances. You can use uvarovite to reduce inflammation or fever.

Personal Protection

Garnet has long been used to guard against physical harm, often being worn in hazardous conditions or during dangerous activities to protect against bodily injury. It is also used in a similar way against toxic influences and unwanted spiritual energies from psychic attacks and those wishing you harm. Wearing melanite around the neck unblocks the heart and throat chakras, allowing the truth to be spoken. Placing spessartite under the pillow wards off nightmares.

Spatial Protection

Garnet revitalizes, purifies, and balances energy. Incorporating it in your closet or personal space boosts inner strength and confidence. Displaying it for all to see unlocks its support in reputation and social harmony. Putting it in the bedroom can attract new relationships and enhance passion.

Personal/Spiritual Growth

Garnet is the birthstone for the month of January. Known as the "stone of commitment," garnet strengthens the survival instinct and is therefore helpful in a crisis or any situation where there seems to be no way out. Andradite stimulates creativity and dissolves feelings of isolation or alienation. Garnet has a strong connection to the pituitary gland and the third eye chakra, the seat of intuition. Placing a garnet, particularly hessonite, on your third eye assists with past-life recall. Hessonite also banishes feelings of guilt and inferiority and encourages self-respect. Pyrope brings stability and vitality in both yourself and relationships. Rhodolite fosters contemplation, intuition, and inspiration.

Hematite

Description

Hematite is the mineral form of ferric oxide, one of the three main oxides of iron. It can be black, silver, or red, and typically has a shiny appearance. The word *hematite* comes from the Greek *haima*, meaning "blood," due to its high iron content and red color. Deposits are found in Canada, Brazil, England, Italy, Switzerland, and Sweden.

History and Lore

According to legend, large hematite deposits formed in locations where ancient battles were fought, as a result of blood being shed and seeping into the earth. Native Americans used powdered hematite to make face paint. Today, ground hematite is still used to make pigments as well as a product called jeweler's rouge, which is used to polish metal.

Uses

Healing Uses

Hematite has long been respected for its benefits to the physical body. It is believed to strengthen the blood supply, encourage the formation of red blood cells, and aid in the absorption of iron. It is also helpful for alleviating circulatory problems and anemia, as well as cleansing the kidneys. Hematite also supports the healing of fractures, and assists with spinal alignment (place a piece at the base and top of the spine for this), and it is believed to draw heat from the body in the case of fever.

Personal Protection

As its mirror-like surface reflects light, hematite is thought to reflect and deflect negative energy, making it a powerful stone of protection. Hematite is also a grounding stone that dissolves negativity, protecting your energy.

Spatial Protection

Hematite is useful for mental clarity and focus, supporting cognitive strength and determination. Placing hematite in areas of the home or office where increased concentration is necessary will assist in clearing mental disruptions and aid in logical thinking. For grounding on the go, keep tumbled hematite stones in your pocket, your car—just about anywhere.

Personal/Spiritual Growth

Due to this stone's ability to reflect and deflect negativity, hematite removes self-imposed limitations and boosts self-esteem and confidence. It is an excellent stone for overcoming compulsions and addictions, as it enhances willpower and survivability. Use hematite during meditation or wear it as a bracelet to calm your thoughts and bring focus and concentration. It strengthens your connection with the earth, particularly during out-of-body experiences. Holding this crystal in deep meditation allows for safe spiritual travel and helps you bring back lessons to use in daily life.

Jade

Description

Jade comes in two forms: jadeite and nephrite. Jadeite is the harder, more highly valued form, and nephrite is softer and more common. Jadeite may be white, light to deep green, blue or blue-green, lavender, orange, or red, while nephrite can be found in creamy white, light to deep green, brown, and black varieties. Jadeite is found in Guatemala, Russia, China, and Myanmar (Burma), and nephrite is found in Guatemala, the Swiss Alps, Russia, China, and New Zealand.

History and Lore

Jade has been an important stone in China going back to the Neolithic period (New Stone Age), when it was first used in burial rituals. During the Han dynasty (206 B.C.E.–C.E. 220), Chinese royalty were buried in jade burial suits to protect them in the afterlife. In Chinese culture, jade is believed to be a link between the physical and spiritual worlds and has long been prized as a carving stone to make jewelry, tools and weapons, and decorative and ceremonial objects.

Uses

Healing Uses

Jade is associated with clarity and purity, and therefore is considered a powerful cleansing stone that supports the filtration and elimination organs of the body, including the kidneys, spleen, and adrenal glands. Using a jade roller on the face or body is thought to improve circulation. Jade is also helpful to the bones and joints, particularly the hips. Jade's restorative property assists in improving infections and helping stitched wounds to bind and heal properly, and it also assists with fertility and childbirth.

Personal Protection

As a travel stone, jade is believed to protect against harm. More generally, jade aids in releasing negative thoughts and calming the mind. Wearing jade around the neck rebalances and unblocks the heart chakra, bringing self-acceptance to the wearer and harmony to tumultuous relationships.

Spatial Protection

Jade is thought to attract wealth and prosperity. Positioning a jade sculpture at the entrance of your home or business welcomes abundance and wards off negative vibrations. Placing jade near your shower assists with deep healing and cleansing of the body when you are at your most vulnerable state. Setting a piece near your bed allows for increased clarity and calmness, giving respite to those with anxiety and repetitive thoughts. Plus, jade is known as the "dream stone"; it can help you remember dreams and release suppressed emotions via dreaming. When placed on the forehead, it brings insightful dreams.

Personal/Spiritual Growth

Jade balances the personality and integrates the mind and body. It encourages you to be yourself and recognize that you are a spiritual being on a human journey. Wearing or holding jade prayer beads or beaded necklaces can be useful in meditation.

Jasper

Description

Jasper is an opaque microcrystalline type of quartz that comes in many varieties and is found worldwide. Its appearance varies widely due to the presence of organic material and mineral inclusions. Leopardskin jasper is named for its spotted look. The patterns of picture jasper look like paintings of landscapes or other scenes from nature. Rainforest jasper (also known as green rhyolite) has a mossy, earthy appearance. Red jasper's vibrant color is a result of its high iron content.

History and Lore

The ancient Egyptians carved jasper amulets and buried their dead with jasper for safe passage to the afterlife. In many cultures, jasper has long been known as the "rain bringer" and is used for the practice of dowsing (searching for water underground). Saint Hildegard of Bingen (1098–1179), a German nun, writer, composer, philosopher, and mystic, wrote of jasper's healing properties and recommended its use to relieve hay fever, cardiac arrhythmia, and temporary deafness.

Uses

Healing Uses

Jasper is a regenerative healing stone. Ocean jasper is referred to as "cellular jasper" for its ability to heal the body on a deep, cellular level. Leopardskin jasper provides support for the muscles and tendons as well as the bones, teeth, and hair. Both picture jasper and rainforest jasper stimulate the immune system and cleanse the kidneys and liver. Red jasper is most popular to wear as jewelry close to the body, as it is renowned for its effects on vitality and assists with blood-related issues and the support of healthy pregnancy and birth. Yellow jasper is closely associated with the solar plexus chakra, and is helpful to carry when you need a boost of energy.

Personal Protection

Jasper is called the "nurturing stone." It provides protective energy during stressful life experiences and ordeals. It is generally considered a talisman that wards off negative energies and grounds the user to the earth's energy during emotional crises. Yellow jasper is believed to protect practitioners during spiritual work as well as travelers on their journeys.

Spatial Protection

Jasper in entranceways and windowsills invites tranquility and repels negative energy. Red jasper in classrooms or spaces of creativity will boost confidence and inspiration. Leopardskin jasper is said to assist with one's relationships with pets, making it an ideal stone to place safely around shared spaces with animal companions.

Personal/Spiritual Growth

Leopardskin jasper grounds your spiritual practice and encourages you to stretch beyond your comfort zone in spiritual matters. You can also use leopardskin jasper to journey into other dimensions with the goal of personal transformation. Picture jasper is said to be the Earth Mother speaking to her children, sending messages from the past through its images. Rainforest jasper can be used to deal with past-life issues. Placed under the pillow, red jasper assists with dream recall. Red jasper can also help you clear your mind for prayer or meditation, and it increases focus and endurance during long spiritual ceremonies or practices. Dalmatian jasper lifts spirits, and can increase inner playfulness.

Lapis Lazuli

Description

Lapis lazuli is composed of several minerals, including lazurite, which gives it its intense blue color, as well as calcite and pyrite, which appear in the stone as white or gold flecks. *Lapis* is the Latin for "stone," and *lazuli* has its roots in Persian and Arabic words that are also the origin for the English word *azure*. This stone is found in the United States, Chile, Argentina, Italy, Afghanistan, Pakistan, and Russia.

History and Lore

Modern-day Afghanistan was the source of lapis lazuli for the ancient Egyptian, Mesopotamian, Greek, and Roman civilizations. For thousands of years, it has been carved to make jewelry and decorative and ceremonial objects, and powdered for use as a pigment. Lapis lazuli is one of the stones used in King Tutankhamun's 3,300-year-old gold burial mask, and the blue turban in Johannes Vermeer's *Girl with a Pearl Earring* (c. 1665) was painted with ultramarine pigment made from powdered lapis lazuli.

Uses

Healing Uses

Lapis lazuli is known as the "wisdom keeper" and is highly regarded for its physical healing benefits. Due to its connection to the third eye chakra (space between eyebrows), it soothes inflammation and provides pain relief, particularly for migraine headaches. It also cares for the throat, larynx, and thyroid, and assists with ear issues, including hearing loss. Lapis lazuli supports the immune system and lowers blood pressure. For eye issues, gently rub the area with a lapis lazuli stone heated in warm water.

Personal Protection

Lapis lazuli opens the third eye and balances the throat chakra. Place this stone at the third eye to enhance psychic abilities, and wear it at the throat to facilitate communication and encourage truth telling. Lapis lazuli is thought to be particularly effective in blocking negative energies from influencing your own perspective. Wearing or holding this stone in environments in which you feel a need to stay true to yourself will assist in making sure you do not become swayed.

Spatial Protection

This blue stone supports tranquility and serenity in the home, making it a perfect addition to any room. Using lapis lazuli as paperweights in the office setting brings balance and clarity to career ambitions. Displaying lapis lazuli around the home fosters peace and healthy communication.

Personal/Spiritual Growth

Lapis lazuli is a truth stone. It is excellent for meditation and spiritual journeying, as it brings harmony and deep inner knowledge. It also encourages self-awareness and helps you discover and accept your innate truth. Hold a tumbled lapis lazuli stone in your hand and listen to your inner voice. Allow its cool, blue essence to release any agitation, frustration, or anger you may be holding inside.

Malachite

Description

Malachite is a green carbonate mineral that typically has a banded appearance and gets its color from its high copper content. Its name most likely derives from its resemblance to the leaves of the mallow plant. Malachite is quite common, with deposits found in Zambia, the Democratic Republic of the Congo, Romania, Russia, and the Middle East.

History and Lore

The ancient Egyptians wore malachite stones as adornments, and they also pulverized the stone and used the powder as eye shadow, as did the Greeks and Romans. In the Middle Ages, malachite was used to guard against the "evil eye" and to cure stomach ailments. Throughout history, many painters have used malachite as a pigment in their work, but that practice has fallen out of favor due to the stone's toxicity in powdered form.

Uses

Healing Uses

Malachite is a powerful stone that provides protection from negative energy as well as pollutants from the atmosphere and other contaminants. (Use malachite only in its polished form, as the dust of the raw form is toxic if inhaled or ingested.) Wearing malachite is believed to ease menstrual cramps and pain during childbirth, and reduce the swelling and inflammation that cause joint and muscle pain. Additionally, this stone has been utilized to alleviate asthma, lower blood pressure, and enhance the immune system.

Personal Protection

Malachite is often thought of as a useful stone to protect against unexplained accidents and mishaps associated with travel. It can break long-held toxic patterns and help you overcome the fear of confrontation when ties need to be cut in relationships. Place malachite on the solar plexus to absorb negative emotions and facilitate deep emotional healing.

Spatial Protection

Malachite absorbs negative energy and pollutants, particularly radiation, and should be cleansed frequently by placing it on a quartz cluster in the sun. Due to its cleansing of electromagnetic pollution, it is especially helpful to keep near microwaves and televisions. In the workplace, malachite can ease the stress of harsh overhead lighting as well as ward off negative energy that might arrive via technology such as emails and phone calls.

Personal/Spiritual Growth

This green stone amplifies positive energy and brings the heart chakra back into balance. It can also be used for scrying (see the Scrying Mirror entry in Chapter 7) or for accessing other worlds. Place malachite on the third eye to enhance psychic vision. Malachite is also a powerful stone of transformation; it encourages risk-taking and brings change. Place it on the heart to bring balance and harmony and foster unconditional love.

Obsidian

Description

Obsidian, also called volcanic glass, is molten lava that cooled so rapidly it had no time to crystallize. It has an opaque, shiny surface and is typically black, but it can also be brown, blue, green, red-black, silver, rainbow, or "gold sheen" if minerals or other inclusions are present. Other types of obsidian include Apache tears and snowflake obsidian. Obsidian is found worldwide wherever there is volcanic activity.

History and Lore

Because of its smooth, curved surface and sharp edges, obsidian has been used to make tools and weapons, especially arrowheads, for thousands of years. It is less common in jewelry because it is not that hard (5 on the Mohs scale) and is easily scratched. Apache tear obsidian gets its name from legend: The US cavalry ambushed a group of Native Americans of the Apache tribe who were camped on a mountain. Three-quarters of the Apaches were killed within minutes, and those who remained, realizing they were outnumbered, chose to leap to their deaths rather than die at the hands of the white men. Their loved ones wept when they discovered their bodies at the base of the mountain, and black stones formed where their tears fell. The legend says that anyone who holds an Apache tear never needs to cry again, because the loved ones of those lost in the fight with the US cavalry have already cried enough tears for all mourners.

Uses

Healing Uses

Obsidian detoxifies the body, aids digestion, and dissolves blockages wherever they occur. When worn as a bracelet or kept bedside overnight, black obsidian is particularly helpful in alleviating the pain of joint problems, cramps, and injuries. Wearing obsidian rings on the fingers may help with arthritis in hands. Apache tear obsidian assists with vitamin absorption. Snowflake obsidian improves circulation.

Personal Protection

Often called a "psychic shield," this stone is used to ward off all negative energy and attacks. Additionally, obsidian is a powerful, cathartic stone. It brings tamped-down negative emotions and unpleasant truths to the surface so they can be dealt with and released. This stone also facilitates past-life healing. A large piece of obsidian can be used to soak up environmental pollution.

Spatial Protection

Obsidian may be placed in doorways to repel negative energy from entering the home. If you find yourself drained when hosting guests, putting it in the entertainment spaces of your home will alleviate fatigue. Because obsidian draws in negative energy, it should be cleansed regularly and should not be placed where it would be forgotten or neglected.

Personal/Spiritual Growth

Obsidian helps you to face your inner darkness and integrate it into your life rather than burying it. Obsidian placed by the bed or under the pillow draws out stress and tension, but once surfaced, the causes of these issues must be resolved. Apache tear or snowflake obsidian works best for this, and stones should be cleansed under running water after use. Black obsidian balls are powerful for meditation and shadow work. Holding this stone while reflecting on dreams assists with recall and interpretation. Place obsidian on the navel to ground spiritual energy in the body. Place it on the third eye to tackle mental barriers.

Onyx

Description

Onyx is a type of chalcedony quartz that has a banded or marble-like appearance and is relatively hard (6.5–7 on the Mohs scale). Most people think of onyx as a black stone, but it also occurs in gray, white, blue, brown, yellow, and red varieties. It is found in many parts of the world, including the United States, Mexico, Brazil, and Italy. The word *onyx* comes from the Greek *onux*, meaning "fingernail."

History and Lore

According to mythology, one day while the goddess of love, Venus, was sleeping, her son, Cupid, cut her fingernails with an arrowhead. The clippings fell into the sand, where they were transformed into stone; having come from part of an immortal being, the stone would never perish. In his 1550 work *De Subtilitate*, the Italian mathematician, physician, astrologer, and philosopher Girolamo Cardano wrote of onyx being used in India to "cool the ardors of love."

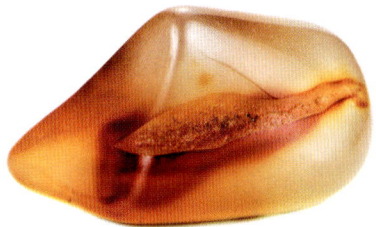

Uses

Healing Uses

Onyx is believed to absorb healing energies from the universe and then transfer them to those in need of healing. Specifically, this stone aids illnesses of the bones and blood, and it is also beneficial for the teeth and feet. Because of its connection to memory, onyx can be used to heal old injuries and physical trauma. Placing this stone in direct contact with the skin increases its effectiveness.

Personal Protection

Onyx is regarded as a shield against negativity and for its connection to the root chakra, which provides grounding while working with the spiritual realms. In this way, onyx offers protection during spiritual counseling, tarot card readings, channeling, or any other practice that invites psychic influences. Place onyx next to your bed to prevent nightmares or night terrors.

Spatial Protection

Onyx can be kept in any room to facilitate a sense of peace and protection. It is especially useful in meditation spaces, where it can provide a safe space for your mind and spirit to confer. Keep onyx on your desk or wherever you work to encourage mental focus and grounding.

Personal/Spiritual Growth

Onyx is said to hold the memories of the wearer, making it useful for past-life work. It also recognizes and reconciles dualities within the self. It anchors those who tend toward erratic behavior and encourages self-control and steadfastness. It supports the concentration necessary to connect with the higher self. In meditation, or throughout the day, hold onyx to overcome fears and anxiety, and to boost wisdom in decision-making.

Opal

Description

Opal is an iridescent mineral of hydrated silica. It is found in an array of colors and varieties, including blue, cherry, chrysopal (blue-green), fire (orange-red), green, and hyalite (clear, glassy). The most famous opal deposits are in Australia, where it is the national gemstone, but it is also found in the United States, Honduras, Brazil, and Slovakia. In 2008, NASA's Mars Reconnaissance Orbiter found opal on Mars, suggesting that liquid water remained on the planet's surface a billion years later than scientists had previously believed.

History and Lore

Australian Aboriginal legend describes the birth of opals: The Creator came down to Earth on a rainbow to bring the message of peace to all humans. On the spot where his foot touched, the stones became vibrant with color and began to sparkle, and this is how opal came to be. Opal plays a role in Sir Walter Scott's 1829 novel *Anne of Geierstein*, in which he writes of "a superb opal, which, amid the changing lights peculiar to that gem, displayed internally a slight tinge of red like a spark of fire."

Uses

Healing Uses

Opal is a stone used to amplify energy in the body, and works with the body to fight infections and purify the blood; cherry opal is believed to be especially helpful for blood disorders. Wear opal jewelry nearest to the parts of your body that require cleansing. Fire opal resonates with the abdomen and lower back, supporting the intestines and kidneys. Green opal strengthens the immune system and battles colds and the flu. Hyalite, also called water opal, combats dehydration and enhances water retention.

Personal Protection

Opal assists with emotional healing and the connection to spiritual realms. Use opal to fortify your energetic shield during vulnerable times of stress and anxiety. Black opal enhances intuition and provides protection during shadow work. Wearing or keeping an opal with you amplifies the positive energy in your aura.

Spatial Protection

The vibrant energy of opal sparks creativity and mental clarity; it is said to bring inspiration and originality to your work. Keeping this stone in a gallery or an art space or on a desk facilitates tapping into the inner muse. Opals on a nightstand assist with emotional intimacy, relationships, and the interpretation of dreams.

Personal/Spiritual Growth

Opal, the birthstone for October, is a delicate stone that supports cosmic consciousness and enhances psychic and mystical visions. Known as the stone of "happy dreams and changes," opal is beneficial while working on self-reflection. It is regarded as a stone of transformation and works closely with the crown and third eye chakras. It assists in revealing emotional information from the past, especially from past lives, and helps to incorporate that information into the present. Blue opal is particularly useful for this; it amplifies and brings to the surface what needs to be seen for deeper examination and provides a positive outlook on moving forward. Wear opal anklets to assist with grounding. Crystal opal in particular opens the mind to new ideas and helps you to see the world with new eyes. Fire opal assists in business matters as well as situations of injustice or mistreatment. Green opal works wonders in relationships.

Rose Quartz

Description

Rose quartz is the pale pink to reddish-pink variety of the mineral quartz, which is composed of silicon dioxide. The pink color is due to the presence of titanium, iron, manganese, or dumortierite in the stone. Rose quartz is found in the United States, Brazil, South Africa, Madagascar, India, and Japan.

History and Lore

The ancient Egyptians believed rose quartz could prevent aging. They used the powdered form in cosmetics to clear the complexion and stop wrinkles, and rose quartz facial masks intended for use in the afterlife have been found in ancient Egyptian tombs. In Greek mythology, this stone is associated with Aphrodite, the goddess of love.

Uses

Healing Uses

Often referred to as the "heart stone," rose quartz's connection to the heart chakra makes it useful for strengthening the heart and circulatory system. Place rose quartz near the thymus gland (just above the heart) to treat chest and lung problems. The stone supports skin regeneration, soothes burns, and clears the complexion. It is also helpful for fertility, pregnancy, and birth issues, and it assists those with Parkinson's, Alzheimer's, or dementia.

Personal Protection

Rose quartz is considered a gentle healer for matters of the heart. This stone is believed to be helpful in drawing love of all forms toward you. In existing relationships, it restores trust and protects unconditional love; in new relationships or dating situations, it acts as protection from heartache. Rose quartz serves as a healing force for old emotional wounds; it helps to ensure that future patterns do not replicate old and unbeneficial ones. Use a rose quartz egg in meditation or as a stone to casually hold in your palm to grow love or enhance fertility.

Spatial Protection

Placing rose quartz by your bed is said to attract love. If this proves too powerful, use it alongside an amethyst to calm things down. Displaying rose quartz in all rooms of the home or office creates a harmonious and uplifting environment. Arranging larger stones on bookshelves or as decor invites this vibration into all areas of your life.

Personal/Spiritual Growth

Rose quartz purifies and opens the heart on all levels, bringing deep inner healing and self-love. It is especially useful when you are finding it hard to forgive or being challenged with your own self-acceptance. Wear the stone over the heart to increase these benefits. For meditation, hold a piece of rose quartz in your "receiving" hand (if you are right-handed, this is your left hand, and vice versa).

Ruby

Description

Ruby is a variety of the mineral corundum (aluminum oxide) that gets its red color from chromium impurities, which make the stone glow under ultraviolet light. The word *ruby* comes from the Latin *rubeus*, meaning "red." This very hard stone (9 on the Mohs scale) is found in many locations worldwide, including Kenya, Madagascar, India, and Myanmar (Burma).

History and Lore

Burma (now Myanmar) has been a major source of rubies since at least C.E. 600. Burmese warriors embedded rubies in their skin for protection during battle. Sanskrit medical texts prescribed rubies as a cure for health issues such as flatulence and stomach pain caused by excess bile. Hindu lore says that a ruby's light cannot be extinguished or hidden by clothing.

Uses

Healing Uses

Ruby is a blood-related stone that stimulates the heart chakra. It detoxifies the blood and benefits the heart and circulatory system. It also alleviates pain associated with menstruation and regulates the menstrual flow. Ruby is helpful during pregnancy, particularly for older women. In fact, this stone is helpful for all issues related to reproduction, including infertility and impotence. Ruby also stimulates the adrenal glands, kidneys, and spleen.

Personal Protection

Throughout history, ruby has been known as the "gemstone of protection," and it can shield against the draining energy or manipulation of others. Wearing ruby jewelry or carrying stones is believed to bring safe travel. Sleeping with a ruby under your pillow brings prophetic dreams and wards off nightmares. Dreaming of rubies indicates prosperity and good fortune—or unexpected guests.

Spatial Protection

Ruby fosters joy and passion, making it a wonderful addition to a space where you entertain guests or spend a significant amount of time. Ruby bowls are particularly helpful in amplifying the energy of the stone to assist in creating a harmonious and inspired vibration.

Personal/Spiritual Growth

Ruby is the birthstone for the month of July. It encourages you to "follow your bliss" and embrace life. This stone's strong connection to the heart chakra promotes motivation and passion. It is helpful for creative and intellectual pursuits, as it sharpens the mind, heightens awareness, and enhances concentration. This stone also balances the energies of the body and invigorates the mind. Wearing ruby is especially helpful for providing a boost of energy when you're feeling lethargic or unmotivated.

Sapphire

Description

Like ruby, sapphire is a variety of the mineral corundum (aluminum oxide). Although sapphire is most recognizable in the blue variety, which gets its color from traces of titanium and iron, this stone can be almost any color, including pink, yellow, and green, as well as colorless. Another variety is star sapphire, with its six-rayed star image or "asterism" caused by the mineral rutile in the stone. Sapphire is found in Madagascar, Sri Lanka, Myanmar (Burma), Australia, and other locations worldwide.

History and Lore

Sri Lanka has been an important source of gemstones for thousands of years and has produced some of the most famous sapphires in the world. The Star of India, exhibited at the American Museum of Natural History in New York City, is a 563-carat star sapphire that is around 2 billion years old. The Logan Sapphire, named after the person who donated it to Washington, DC's Smithsonian National Museum of Natural History in 1960, is a 423-carat sapphire about the size of an egg, mounted in a silver and gold brooch setting and surrounded by twenty brilliant-cut diamonds. For centuries, sapphires have been associated with royalty, a recent example of which is the sapphire engagement ring Prince Charles gave to Diana, now worn by Kate Middleton, Princess of Wales.

Uses

Healing Uses

Sapphire regulates the glands and treats blood disorders, and it also helps with sleep issues, such as insomnia. Green sapphire may heal eye infections and improve eyesight. Blue sapphire connects with the throat chakra and is believed to heal the thyroid; wear it around the neck to increase these benefits. Yellow sapphire removes toxins from the body. Soaking sapphire in spring water for a few hours, removing the stone, then using the water to make tea or adding it to bathwater will enhance the healing properties of this stone.

Personal Protection

Sapphire is regarded for its ability to purify the aura, allowing for negative energies to be dispelled. Additionally, it has the power to amplify positive energies, and provide a space for positive vibrations to flow freely. Sapphire is an excellent stone to dispel psychic attacks from undesired energies. Green sapphire enhances physical vision, improves inner vision, and assists in dream recall. Wear blue sapphire at the throat to release frustration and facilitate self-expression. Star sapphire is said to enable a connection with extraterrestrial beings, while indigo and blue hues of this stone are believed to be conduits to guardian angels.

Spatial Protection

Sapphire is known as the "plenty stone" because of its connection to monetary abundance for those who utilize its properties. Placing this stone in an area of your house already dedicated to budgeting and finances is said to assist with reaching your fiscal goals. Sapphire is also helpful in dealing with difficult memories and emotions, making it a lovely stone to place in a therapist's office or your home's spaces of reflection.

Personal/Spiritual Growth

Sapphire is the birthstone for the month of September. This stone brings peace of mind and serenity as well as spiritual power. Known to stimulate the throat chakra, it stimulates self-expression. Use sapphire for self-exploration and to increase confidence. Hold it in meditation to illuminate spiritual truths, as it is known for its ability to attract favor from the divine.

Selenite

Description

Selenite is composed of calcium sulfate dihydrate and is a crystallized form of the mineral gypsum. These soft rocks are slightly flexible, and have a transparent to milky white hue. Formed through the evaporation of mineral-rich water, they are some of the largest crystals ever found. The largest to date weighs more than 55 tons and is in the Cave of the Crystals in Mexico.

History and Lore

Selenite has been revered by humans for thousands of years. The ancient Greeks named it after Selene, the goddess of the moon, due to its luminescent appearance. It was even used to make windows because of its translucent properties, adding to its symbolism. While traditional selenite is a clear or milky hue, different colors occur when it forms crystals with other minerals. Green selenite occurs in southern Australia when forming with copper, while desert rose selenite is found in Morocco due to the inclusion of sand.

Uses

Healing Uses

This stone is highly regarded for its benefits in skeletal health, specifically spinal alignment and the absorption of calcium in the bones. It is thought to aid with mental clarity, both in brain health as well as relief from chronic anxiety. It is known for its ability to reverse the effects of free radicals, assisting in the maintenance of healthy skin, hair, and eyes. Able to heal the body on a cellular level, consistent usage of this crystal contributes to a brighter physical appearance.

Personal Protection

Selenite is able to dispel negative thoughts and energies. It is well known to cleanse the aura, as it wards off lower vibrations and reduces stress. This crystal clears blockages in your energy field left over from daily interpersonal interactions. This stone is renowned for its unique protection from the harm of electromagnetic fields (EMF). EMF vibrations given off by technology are all around us, and can contribute to brain fog, dizziness, and insomnia.

Spatial Protection

The unique ability to transmute negative energies makes this a perfect stone to place in each of the four corners of your home. In addition, placing a stick of selenite above the main entrance will assist in cleansing the vibrations of all who enter. It is capable of swiftly removing stagnant and ill-humored energy, which makes it ideal for keeping near to where you sleep, work, or spend most of your time.

Personal/Spiritual Growth

This crystal is beneficial for all types of relationships. It promotes healthy communication and honest interactions, and heals past wounds. Working with this stone allows you to open up your mind and heart to the messages from the spiritual realm and higher self as it energizes the crown chakra (the space at the top of your head known to welcome spiritual messages). This stone supports experiences like connecting you with your gifts as well as understanding your life purpose.

Smoky Quartz

Description

Smoky quartz is a light to dark brown variety of quartz whose color and smoky appearance are caused by aluminum impurities and either natural or artificial irradiation of the stone. This stone is found in many locations in the world, including the United States, Brazil, Madagascar, and Australia. Cairngorm is a variety of smoky quartz crystal found in Scotland's Cairngorm Mountains.

History and Lore

Smoky quartz is the national gem of Scotland and has been important in that region of the world going back to the time of the Druids, whose earliest known records date back to the third century B.C.E. The stone was used to make sunglasses in China in the twelfth century.

Uses

Healing Uses

Smoky quartz is very effective for pain relief, particularly headaches and muscle cramps. To activate this purpose, place a crystal on the painful spot with the point directed away from the body. This stone also regulates the fluids within the body and assists in the absorption of minerals. Because smoky quartz is irradiated, it is excellent for relieving radiation-related issues and easing the negative effects of sunburn and medical radiation therapies. However, be sure to select naturally formed stones rather than ones that have been artificially irradiated (artificially irradiated stones are usually darker in color, almost black and leaning toward opaque).

Personal Protection

Smoky quartz neutralizes negative vibrations, guards against geopathic stress, and absorbs electromagnetic smog. Keeping it while driving also protects against road rage. Smoky quartz's connection to the root chakra makes it a powerful stress reliever because it brings strength and stability. To protect yourself from stress, hold a stone in each hand and sit quietly for a few moments.

Spatial Protection

Known as an amulet of protection, situating smoky quartz around your valuables, in a car, and around a home's entryways guards against theft. Placing a circle of these crystals around your desk or work area protects your environment from negative workplace gossip, toxic managers, and general interference, allowing for a safe space in which to concentrate.

Personal/Spiritual Growth

This stone has a strong connection to the root chakra, located at the base of the spine, which is your anchor in the natural world. Its grounding spiritual energy makes it excellent for meditation. Smoky quartz is also regarded for its ability to bring the ethereal into the physical world, making it a useful stone to experience otherworldly phenomena such as ghosts, fairies, and extraterrestrial communication.

Tiger's Eye

Description

Tiger's eye is a type of quartz that is typically yellow-brown in color but can also be pink, red, or blue. It has a banded appearance and a silky sheen, due to its fibrous structure. Sources of tiger's eye include the United States, South Africa, India, and Australia. Tiger iron is a related stone, composed of tiger's eye, red jasper, and black hematite. Blue or blue-gray tiger's eye is called hawk's eye or falcon's eye.

History and Lore

For thousands of years, the various "eye" stones have been considered strong talismans with an "all-seeing" power. The ancient Egyptians used the stone for the eyes in statues of gods. Roman soldiers carried tiger's eye for courage and protection in battle.

Uses

Healing Uses

Tiger's eye is thought to boost the endocrine system, bringing balance to hormones. Red tiger's eye speeds up a slow metabolism. Regarded as a blood fortifier, hawk's eye aids the circulatory system, bowels, and legs. Tiger's eye supports eye issues and enhances vision, and it also assists with neck and spinal problems. Place a tiger's eye stone on either side of the head to rebalance the brain's hemispheres, encouraging an improvement in depression symptoms.

Personal Protection

As an ancient talisman, tiger's eye is said to be an "all-seeing, all-knowing eye," and thought to give the wearer the power of observation. It is used to protect against negative energy from outside forces. It allows insight into others' motivations and provides knowledge and clarity.

Spatial Protection

Place tiger's eye near the front door or a large window to take advantage of its protective qualities. It is regarded as a stone of great luck, and is especially supportive to new businesses and ventures. Display tiger's eye in spaces where creative talents are tested to grow something new.

Personal/Spiritual Growth

This stone helps in solving problems and resolving conflicts, and it also unblocks creativity. Placed on the third eye, this stone enhances psychic abilities and balances the lower chakras. Hawk's eye assists with clairvoyance. Set tiger's eye on the solar plexus/navel chakra for spiritual grounding. Red tiger's eye is a stimulating stone that battles lethargy and boosts motivation, helping you locate inner resources and accomplish your goals. Wear a tiger's eye bracelet to reduce the cravings for foods or when quitting smoking/vaping as it helps overcome discouragement and assists with working through lifestyle changes.

Topaz

Description

Topaz is a transparent silicate mineral of aluminum and fluorine that is quite hard (8 on the Mohs scale). It is most recognizable as a golden-yellow stone, but other varieties include brown, blue, pink, green, and colorless. Deposits of topaz have been found in the United States, Mexico, Pakistan, Sri Lanka, and Australia.

History and Lore

Up until the eleventh century, the word *topaz* (which comes from *Topazios*, the ancient Greeks' name for an island in the Red Sea) was used to describe green gemstones. (Topazios was also a source of the green gem peridot.) However, in his *Liber lapidum* (Book of Stones), Marbodus of Rennes (c. 1035–1123) stated that the color of topaz is yellow, and from then on this is how the stone was known. The twelfth-century German nun, writer, composer, philosopher, and mystic Saint Hildegard of Bingen (1098–1179) wrote about the healing powers of topaz soaked in wine.

Uses

Healing Uses

Topaz is a wonderful healing stone held in high esteem for manifesting overall well-being. It is thought to fortify the nervous system and aid digestion. It is believed to also stimulate metabolism, and be a gentle support to those suffering eating disorders such as anorexia and bulimia. Blue topaz assists with issues related to the throat and vocal cords. Known for its ability to liven up taste buds, topaz is excellent for those who have lost their sense of taste. Carefully sucking on a topaz before a meal allows for improved food appreciation and digestion.

Personal Protection

The soothing effects of topaz make it supportive in affirmation, manifestation, and visualization practices, as it is known to boost faith and protect against self-doubt. Use topaz to make requests of the universe that you hope will manifest on the earth plane. In the form of an amulet, topaz alleviates sadness and mood swings. Wearing blue topaz on a chain or holding it in a pouch assists children with the emotional pain of bullying. Topaz is thought to shield against psychic attacks, making it a great stone to carry around when you feel someone has a vendetta against you.

Spatial Protection

Topaz has a vibrant energy that replaces negativity with love and joy. This stone is most powerful when placed in the heart of the home, like the kitchen or main living area, as it promotes well-being and healing in all areas of family life.

Personal/Spiritual Growth

Along with citrine, topaz is a birthstone for the month of November. It is a mellow, empathetic stone that promotes truth and forgiveness. When feeling disorganized, place a golden topaz in one hand and blue topaz in the other to balance logic and intuition. When placed on the throat or third eye, topaz enhances the personal voice. Clear topaz is especially helpful for use in animal communication. Use blue topaz during meditation to access the higher self. Holding pink topaz helps to break old patterns.

Tourmaline

Description

Tourmaline is a crystalline silicate mineral containing aluminum, boron, and other elements. It is found in almost every color, including multicolored (elbaite) and pink-and-green "watermelon" varieties, but the most common type is iron-rich black tourmaline, also known as schorl. Tourmaline is found in the United States, Brazil, Africa, Afghanistan, and Sri Lanka.

History and Lore

When tourmaline was first mined, no distinction was made between it and other gemstones. Throughout history, "rubies" were often misidentified red tourmaline stones, and green tourmaline was often mistaken for emerald. Today, tourmaline is recognized and appreciated in its own right, and was popularized in the United States beginning in the late 1800s when Tiffany gemologist George F. Kunz praised the stones found in Maine and California.

Uses

Healing Uses

The striations in a tourmaline crystal enhance energy flow, making this an excellent healing stone, particularly in wand form. Blue tourmaline is useful for identifying the underlying causes of a disease. Yellow tourmaline focuses on the digestive and cleansing organs of the body, including the stomach, liver, spleen, kidneys, and gallbladder. Red tourmaline heals the heart and blood vessels. Watermelon tourmaline helps to regenerate the nerves.

Personal Protection

Tourmaline is a shamanic stone that provides protection during meditation and spiritual rituals. When connecting with the ethereal realms, holding this stone is helpful in bringing your energy back down to the physical plane. Wear black tourmaline to protect against electromagnetic smog and radiation, and to act as a shield to all negative energy.

Spatial Protection

Red tourmaline boosts passion, making these stones great additions to the bedroom. Black tourmaline is known for its ability to block electromagnetic pollution, and it can be set next to Wi-Fi towers, computers, and other technological devices. Keeping green tourmaline in the bedrooms of young children promotes growth and healthy development.

Personal/Spiritual Growth

This stone is highly regarded among spiritual practitioners; it is often called the "receptive stone" as it promotes wisdom and peace in many mystical practices. Blue tourmaline brings psychic awareness and facilitates visions. Brown tourmaline is an excellent grounding stone that also clears the aura. Watermelon tourmaline activates the heart chakra, providing a link to the higher self and promoting love, tenderness, and friendship. Green tourmaline inspires creativity. Black tourmaline clears negative thoughts and fosters a laid-back, positive attitude, regardless of the circumstances.

Turquoise

Description

Turquoise is an opaque mineral that is found in various shades of blue and green, due to the copper in its composition. The word *turquoise* comes from the Old French *turqueise*, meaning "Turkish." The stone is found in the United States, Mexico, France, Egypt, the Middle East, Russia, Peru, and China.

History and Lore

This stone gets its name from the incorrect belief that it came from Turkey. Though turquoise was traded in Turkey, it was imported from other places, mainly Iran and the Sinai Peninsula. The ancient Egyptians, Sumerians, and Aztecs prized turquoise, and some Native American tribes consider turquoise a sacred stone that connects earth and heaven.

Uses

Healing Uses

Turquoise calms the emotions and promotes feelings of peace and well-being. It is thought to be a helpful stone to address the effects of inflammation. It can help to balance mood swings, reduce stress, and ease depression. Its purifying properties can aid detoxification and protect against environmental pollution. Turquoise aligns with the throat and heart chakras; therefore, wearing it as a necklace can enhance communication, soothe throat complaints, and lessen emotional suffering.

Personal Protection

This stone offers protection against physical, psychic, and environmental harm. Turquoise can also be worn or carried to encourage emotional and physical well-being as well as clear the mind from turbulent thoughts. When worn or carried, it brings good fortune and abundance.

Spatial Protection

Place a piece of turquoise where you will see it often as a reminder to prioritize your wellness goals. Putting it in the bathroom, bedroom, and other deeply personal spaces clarifies the energy and promotes a serene, balanced atmosphere. Display this stone wherever you need improved communication, such as a living area or office meeting space.

Personal/Spiritual Growth

Considered connected to the earth's oceans, turquoise promotes serenity and self-healing, making it a perfect stone for prioritizing self-care. Meditate while holding turquoise to improve your connection with the spiritual realm. As it strengthens the emotions, turquoise helps you gain confidence and release self-limiting behaviors. It can also reduce feelings of loneliness and isolation, enabling you to realize a deeper link with "all that is."

2

The Power of Herbs
and Spices

Plants have long been a cornerstone of wellness. They're connected to the energy of the earth through their roots, and they offer a bounty of healing properties, from soothing colds to aiding digestion. These herbs and plants are manifestations of Mother Nature and can be cherished companions on your path to energetic wellness. Although Western society has largely stopped using plants for medicinal purposes, they can sometimes be more effective, less expensive, and safer than their pharmaceutical counterparts.

In energy healing, specific plants and herbs work with the life energy of the individual, correcting imbalances and allowing for fundamental healing beyond the physical body. As living beings themselves, herbs bestow their own energies to amplify, repair, and connect us within a natural state of flow, and utilizing them validates the role of the spiritual body in facilitating physical health. Herbs contribute to the health of the life force energy by supporting the physical body's natural rhythms and healing mechanisms, allowing for a more comprehensive restoration.

Nature provides an abundance of ways for you to use herbs to heal your body and mind. Depending on the plant, you can use the leaves, flowers, berries, and/or roots in fresh, dried, or powdered form. Boiling chamomile flowers makes a gentle tea to alleviate fevers, and burning ginseng root or powder as incense can repel negativity. The more than two dozen herbs in this chapter can bring you in touch with the natural world while boosting your well-being.

Generally speaking, herbs are natural and healthy and safe, but if you are taking any prescription medications, be sure to consult your doctor before experimenting with herbal remedies, as this could result in negative interactions. Also, some herbs, such as valerian, can be habit-forming if taken in large quantities or for prolonged periods of time. Start small, work with a licensed practitioner to choose options, and pay attention to your body's responses. If something doesn't work for you, try something else. There are plenty of herbs out there!

Angelica

Description

Angelica is an herb in the parsley family. The plant is tall, with large compound umbrella-like sprays of white or greenish flowers. The stems can be candied and eaten, and the roots can be used for flavoring liqueurs. Angelica is native to temperate and subarctic regions of the Northern Hemisphere, including Norway, Lithuania, and Russia. Its name comes from the Greek *angelos*, meaning "messenger" or "angel."

History and Lore

According to legend, an angel came to a monk in a dream to reveal a plant that would cure the plague (hence the name). Angelica is one of the main ingredients in Carmelite water, a lemon balm–based tonic created by Carmelite monks in the 1600s to cure headaches, promote relaxation, and protect the drinker against poisons and spells. A related herb called Chinese angelica, or dong quai, has been used in Chinese medicine for thousands of years.

Uses

Healing Uses

Angelica is used to cure fevers, colds, and coughs, and it is particularly effective as an expectorant to clear chest congestion. It is also helpful for bringing on menstruation and relieving bloating or cramps; pregnant women should not use angelica, as it could cause a miscarriage. Angelica contains compounds that are used to aid conditions such as high blood pressure, migraines, and Raynaud's disease.

Personal Protection

Associated with angels and divinity, angelica is highly regarded for providing an aura of protection. It centers energy and creates a fortified energetic shield, allowing for safe exploration during vulnerable spiritual and emotional frames of mind. Adding to a bath or carrying in a pouch provides you with a comforting force of protection.

Spatial Protection

Angelica protects against negative energy and attracts positive energy and therefore is a good addition to spiritual spaces. Angelica root can be added to potpourri and placed all around your living space for protection. Grow angelica in the garden to protect the home. Sprinkle dried angelica leaves in the four corners of the home to ward off negativity. Burn dried angelica leaves to rid yourself of old patterns. Add angelica to bathwater to remove unwanted psychic attachments.

Personal/Spiritual Growth

Angelica provides a deep connection to the divine, and is especially healing in times of loss and heartache. It relaxes the mind and stimulates the imagination. It is known to offer strength and balance during threshold experiences, such as death and childbirth and other life passages, and is especially helpful during difficult times when you feel cut off from your inner self. As an essential oil, angelica has a revitalizing effect, making it useful for a boost during a sluggish period.

Arnica

Description

Arnica is a perennial herb in the Asteraceae or Compositae family, which also includes asters, daisies, and sunflowers. The *Arnica montana* species has yellow or orange flowers, and the flowers and roots are dried and used for medicinal and other purposes. *Arnica montana* is native to Europe and Siberia, but other species in the *Arnica* genus also grow in North America, particularly in mountainous regions.

History and Lore

Arnica has several nicknames, including wolf's bane (which it confusingly shares with aconite) and mountain tobacco. Though it has a long history of medicinal use in many cultures, it was especially popular in Germany. The German writer Johann Wolfgang von Goethe (1749–1832), who suffered from angina, credited arnica with saving his life.

Uses

Healing Uses

Dried arnica flowers placed in bathwater will ease general aches and pains. When added to massage oil, arnica relieves muscle soreness, swelling, and inflammation. Arnica should not be placed directly on an open wound; instead, place a compress of dried flowers and roots over a bandaged wound for pain relief and to aid the healing process. This herb should be taken internally only under the supervision of a certified herbalist, as it can cause gastrointestinal distress and other negative reactions.

Personal Protection

Arnica provides energetic boundaries when scattered and grown. Keeping an arnica plant in a space where you often find yourself deep in thought will assist with clearing your mind. Scattering a bit under your pillow allows for a peaceful sleep, free from the infiltration of unwanted energy.

Spatial Protection

This herb is also associated with the harvest and can be used in the garden to boost its growing power. For protection from negative energy, add the dried flowers to boiling water to make a tea, and then sprinkle the liquid around the door and window frames of the home.

Personal/Spiritual Growth

Known to be connected to the element of fire, this herb can open up intuition and passion. Arnica flowers increase psychic powers, expanding the channels of connection to spiritual realms. Meditate with arnica essence to release pent-up pain from past trauma, gain wisdom, and move forward in a balanced, harmonized way. Arnica essential oil can be used in aromatherapy to promote positivity and gratitude.

Basil

Description

Basil (*Ocimum basilicum*) is an aromatic annual herb in the mint family that is native to Africa and Asia. The word *basil* comes from the Greek *basilikos*, meaning "royal." A variant called holy basil, or tulsi, is native to India and plays an important role in the Hindu religion.

History and Lore

In ancient Greece, basil was associated with grief and mourning. In sixteenth-century Europe, it had a curious connection: It was believed that scorpions were attracted to basil and that a basil sprig left under a pot containing a basil plant would turn into a scorpion. A French doctor once wrote that smelling basil would cause a scorpion to grow in the brain.

Uses

Healing Uses

As a tea, basil relieves stomach pain, cramps, indigestion, and constipation; eases migraines; and stimulates lactation in nursing mothers. The herb also has antibacterial and antifungal properties (use the oil for best results in these cases).

Personal Protection

Basil is known as a protective herb and can be used to ward off negative energy. Make your own powerful smoke cleansing stick by bundling dried basil, then carefully burn the end of the stick to cleanse a space. It is also a useful herb to attune the heart to new relationships as well as strengthen old ones. Keeping a pot of this herb close to you and using its leaves in tea, oils, and aromatherapy can assist with attracting love.

Spatial Protection

Known as an herb of purification, you may burn basil as incense to cleanse a home of negativity. Given as a gift, basil brings good luck to a new home. Keeping a pot of basil in your home is said to attract wealth and prosperity.

Personal/Spiritual Growth

Basil brings courage and strength to those who are fearful and helps to clear clouded judgment. It also eases anxiety and improves communication. Its reassuring aroma can even be a bridge between the physical and spiritual realms. Use holy basil for prayer and meditation or to enhance memory. Place basil in bathwater to get over an old love or to invite new love in. (See the Basil entry in Chapter 4 to learn about the additional benefits of basil essential oil.)

Bay Laurel

Description

Bay laurel (*Laurus nobilis*) is an aromatic evergreen tree, native to the Mediterranean region, that produces the bay leaf commonly used in cooking. The leaves can be used fresh or dried (fresh is stronger) but should be removed before serving because they are difficult to digest. A bay leaf placed in a container of rice or flour is thought to deter pests.

History and Lore

In ancient times, a wreath of laurel was given as a sign of honor or victory (hence the term *laureate*). To "rest on one's laurels" is to rely on past successes for future fame or recognition. The Greek god Apollo is always depicted wearing a laurel wreath on his head to represent his love for the nymph Daphne, whose father turned her into a laurel tree to protect her from Apollo's advances.

Uses

Healing Uses

Bay laurel oil can be used with massage to soothe muscle aches and pains. As a salve, bay laurel soothes bruises, itching, and minor skin irritations. A tea made of the leaves and berries aids digestion and has a calming effect. Adding bay laurel to bathwater assists with healing after childbirth. Carefully burn bay leaves to purify a space following an illness.

Personal Protection

The strong scent of the bay laurel leaf makes it very effective in purification rituals, especially cleansing a space. Mixed with sandalwood, it is useful for clearing disharmonious energy. Place bay laurel in your pillowcase to encourage sound sleep and induce prophetic dreams, and carrying a few leaves around with you protects against unwanted energy throughout your day.

Spatial Protection

Place bay laurel leaves at the entrances to your home or office to ward off unwanted guests and attention. Create a jar or bowl filled with bay laurel leaves, salt, and other herbs you find comforting and place intermittently around your living area to magnify the protection and purification this herb brings.

Personal/Spiritual Growth

Using bay laurel during meditation amplifies clairvoyance, as it is associated with divination and intuition. It also heightens awareness and perception. Burn a candle dressed with bay laurel oil to bring about personal change. Write a wish or desire on a bay leaf and then burn it to make the wish come true. Use bay laurel essential oil on your body to boost confidence, encourage inspiration, and promote creativity.

Black Cohosh

Description

Black cohosh (*Actaea racemosa*) is a plant in the buttercup (Ranunculaceae) family with tall, white flowering racemes (flower stalks). A perennial plant, it is native to North America and typically grows in woodland areas. Other names for black cohosh include black snakeroot, due to its history as a snakebite remedy, and black bugbane, because it is known to repel insects. A related plant, blue cohosh, has similar attributes.

History and Lore

Native Americans have used black cohosh for centuries to treat a number of conditions, including gynecological issues, kidney problems, headaches, and depression. In nineteenth-century America, the plant was used as a home remedy for rheumatism and fever, as a diuretic, and to bring on menstruation.

Uses

Healing Uses

Black cohosh, which contains a compound thought to have estrogen-like activity, is used to soothe hot flashes, night sweats, and other symptoms of menopause. For this reason, it is often prescribed as an alternative to estrogen replacement therapy (also called hormone replacement therapy). It also eases premenstrual tension and cramps. Black cohosh is occasionally used to treat skin conditions such as acne and for healing following wart or mole removal. It can also be used to ease rheumatism, lung conditions, and neurological issues. Due to its interactions with hormones, always consult with a medical professional for recommendations on dosage.

Personal Protection

Black cohosh is especially helpful in draining and emotional situations, as it provides a barrier against unwanted spiritual intrusions. Because of its ability to kick-start spiritual renewal, you can carry black cohosh in your pocket to protect your courage, faith, and determination. Used in a sachet, black cohosh preserves and protects existing love or invites new love into your life.

Spatial Protection

Black cohosh is a protective plant. Sprinkle it around the home, burn as incense, or use the tea as a floor wash to keep evil and negative influences at bay.

Personal/Spiritual Growth

Black cohosh assists with transformation. Its black roots represent darkness in the past, and its white flowers are the promise of a bright future. Use this herb to release yourself from old attachments and move confidently forward into a new phase of your life. Added to bathwater, it brings courage.

Black Pepper

Description

This pungent spice comes from the pepper plant (*Piper nigrum*), which is native to south India but also grows in other parts of the world, particularly tropical regions. The small, unripe fruits of this plant are dried (as peppercorns) and ground to make the spice found in household pepper shakers.

History and Lore

Dubbed "black gold," black pepper has been used in India for thousands of years. The ancient Egyptians also used this spice. The Egyptian pharaoh Ramesses II (1301–1213 B.C.E.) was entombed with black peppercorns in his nostrils, most likely for preservation and to maintain the shape of his nose.

Uses

Healing Uses

Black pepper has powerful digestive properties. The aroma and spicy flavor of black pepper trigger the stomach to produce hydrochloric acid, which is needed to digest protein, and they also stimulate the pancreas to produce important digestive enzymes. Piperine, the alkaloid that makes black pepper so pungent, has antioxidant qualities. In Western herbalism, black pepper is used in cold and flu remedies. In Ayurvedic medicine, black pepper is mixed with honey to reduce respiratory congestion.

Personal Protection

As a powerful protective herb, black pepper banishes negativity and protects against negativity and unwanted energetic interference. Carry black pepper with you to banish feelings of jealousy and to protect yourself from the jealousy of others. When feeling the negative influence of others infiltrating your sacred mental space, using pepper with intention while cooking breaks the energetic chords you no longer wish to house. Place peppercorns in a pouch and place under your pillow to discourage bad dreams and unwanted energies invading your peaceful space.

Spatial Protection

Black pepper is useful for cleansing a previously occupied home for a new owner. Crush the peppercorns and add them to a smoke cleansing stick before burning.

Personal/Spiritual Growth

Black pepper is wonderful for relieving anxiety and stress. It encourages you to release those negative influences and find your inner source of power. Consuming black pepper in food helps you "digest" unhealthy feelings toward yourself and others, while providing the courage and stamina needed to get through the process and move forward. Black pepper essential oil has various health benefits, such as supporting digestion and soothing sore muscles, and it can also be used in aromatherapy to boost energy.

Calendula

Description

Calendula (*Calendula officinalis*), more commonly known as marigold, is a flowering plant native to the Mediterranean region. The word *calendula* comes from the Latin *kalendae*, meaning "calends," the first day of the month in the ancient Roman calendar. The more common name, marigold, is a reference to the Virgin Mary.

History and Lore

According to legend, a Greek maiden named Caltha fell in love with Apollo, the sun god. Consumed by her love, she waited in the fields all night, hoping to catch first sight of him in the morning. Eventually she wasted away and died, and a marigold, bright yellow like the sun, appeared in the place where she had stood. In India, marigolds are sacred to the goddess Mahadevi and are worn as garlands at the festival honoring her.

Uses

Healing Uses

Place a compress saturated with warm calendula tea on wounds and skin inflammations, including rashes and insect bites. You can also use calendula essential oil for this purpose, as it has a gentle, cooling effect. Taken internally, calendula cleanses the lymph system and aids in healing ulcers. This plant also relieves pain associated with menstruation and is a common addition to salves aiding in all sorts of ailments. One way to enjoy the herb's health benefits is to use it as a substitute for saffron in dishes such as yellow rice.

Personal Protection

Calendula and its vibrant golden petals carried in a pouch are helpful for lifting spirits and warding off malevolent forces. Adding marigold petals to bathwater assists with career aspirations, as well as with cleansing your energy in order to become more receptive to opportunity.

Spatial Protection

Wreaths of marigold hung over a doorway are said to keep evil and negativity from entering a home. Sprinkle marigold petals on the floor under the bed to invite prophetic dreams. Rolling a candle in calendula before lighting it will amplify its protective properties when displayed about the home.

Personal/Spiritual Growth

Calendula is thought to carry the healing energy of the sun, and projects a warm, healing light of comfort to those who are fearful, nervous, or recovering from the shock of a trauma. It encourages understanding and compassion and tempers anger and rash behavior. In meditation, anointing yourself with calendula-infused oil brings clarity, and you can also burn marigold petals as incense for divination.

Cayenne

Description

Cayenne pepper is a hot chili pepper that is commonly used in its dried or powdered form to flavor dishes. It is a member of the genus *Capsicum*, which also includes bell peppers, jalapeños, and others. This pepper is native to the Americas and gets its name from the capital city of French Guiana.

History and Lore

Records show that cayenne pepper was in use in Central and South America as early as 8000 B.C.E. Christopher Columbus introduced the pepper to Europe in the late fifteenth century. The American herbalist and botanist Samuel Thomson (1769–1843) created an alternative system of medicine that included cayenne pepper in many of its remedies to restore the body's inner heat.

Uses

Healing Uses

Cayenne pepper is a go-to herb to alleviate headaches, colds, and the flu. It is also used to address digestive and intestinal problems, including ulcers. Used in foods, cayenne boosts the metabolism and circulation and benefits the heart. It is also used to help lower blood pressure. Used as a counterirritant in salves or dissolved in bathwater, it soothes such conditions as rheumatism and arthritis. When combined with lemon juice and honey, cayenne cleanses the body of toxins and poisons, and supports the immune system.

Personal Protection

Heighten your spiritual awareness by inhaling the scent of cayenne-infused oils. Lighting a candle anointed with cayenne can amplify an intention you set while doing so, as it boosts personal strength and shields against draining energies.

Spatial Protection

Encircle your meditation area or reflective space with a sprinkling of cayenne to repel negative energies. Scatter cayenne pepper around your home, especially in doorways and thresholds between rooms to eliminate stagnant energy, and establish a spiritual balance.

Personal/Spiritual Growth

Cayenne pepper energizes the spirit by energizing the body. This process brings heightened spiritual awareness of the invisible world. Incorporating it into a morning beverage can act as a spiritual stimulant, readying yourself to meet the day with optimism, focus, and motivation. Cayenne can also be added to dishes to bring spice and heat to romantic relationships, or to cope with the pain of separation or divorce. This spice balances the heart chakra.

Chamomile

Description

Native to Europe and the Mediterranean, chamomile is an aromatic perennial herb in the Asteraceae family. The most commonly used variety is German chamomile (*Matricaria recutita* or *Matricaria chamomilla*). The flowers of the chamomile plant are its most useful part; with white petals and yellow centers, they bear a strong resemblance to daisies. This plant's name comes from the Greek *khamaimelon: khamai*, meaning "on the ground," and *melon*, meaning "apple."

History and Lore

Chamomile was used for medicinal purposes in the ancient Egyptian, Greek, and Roman civilizations. Greek physicians prescribed it for fevers and female issues. In her 1911 book *The Herb Garden*, Frances A. Bardwell praises chamomile for the positive effect it has on other plants. Roman chamomile (*Chamaemelum nobile*) is used to flavor Spanish sherry.

Uses

Healing Uses

Chamomile is a calming herb that reduces stress. Drink chamomile tea to ease stomach discomfort and aid digestion, or to relax in the evening and ensure a good night's sleep. To alleviate symptoms of fevers, colds, and the flu, combine dried chamomile flowers with boiling water and inhale the steam for up to ten minutes. Chamomile tea can also be applied externally, to treat burns, skin infections, and hemorrhoids. Chamomile essential oil soothes sore muscles following exercise.

Personal Protection

To eliminate stuck or heavy energy, steep chamomile in warm water, sprinkle with basil, and drink as a tea. Bathing in chamomile and sea salt can cleanse the aura from unwanted energies.

Spatial Protection

Spread dried chamomile flowers around the home to ward off negative influences and provide protection. You may even brew a strong chamomile tea and mist it around the home to provide a metaphysical barrier of protection.

Personal/Spiritual Growth

Chamomile has a soothing, sedating effect that is helpful when you are experiencing anxiety, going through a difficult time, or recovering from a traumatic experience. Because chamomile creates abundance, it is especially useful for manifesting money. Inhaling chamomile is thought to bring peace of mind to meditation sessions. Burning chamomile incense, or diffusing its oil, before intention setting allows the mind to align to a high vibrational state. Add chamomile to bathwater to attract love. Washing your hands in chamomile water is said to increase luck. When your mind won't shut off, this herb has a quieting effect that can bring calm and comfort.

Cinnamon

Description

Cinnamon is the dried inner bark of certain tropical Asian trees of the genus *Cinnamomum*. It is most commonly used in stick or powdered form to add flavor to foods and beverages, but it also has various medicinal and protective uses. Sri Lanka is a major source of cinnamon, as are Indonesia and China.

History and Lore

Cinnamon has been used in Chinese medicine for more than 4,000 years. In ancient Egypt, it was not only consumed; it was also used in embalming practices. Legend has it that the Roman emperor Nero (37–68) burned all the cinnamon he could find on the funeral pyre of his second wife, Poppaea Sabina, to punish himself for his role in her death. Cinnamon is mentioned in the Bible as an ingredient in anointing oil.

Uses

Healing Uses

Cinnamon relieves stomach discomfort, including morning sickness and motion sickness, and can be used to treat digestive problems such as gas, diarrhea, and vomiting. It can be brewed into a tea, and also taken as a supplement. Cinnamon is also useful for soothing sore throats, coughs, colds, headaches, and the flu. In Ayurvedic medicine, cinnamon is used as a remedy for diabetes.

Personal Protection

Cinnamon relates to the element of fire and is therefore extra powerful when burned. Burn cinnamon as incense to invite love, cleanse and protect your vibration, and heighten psychic awareness. Cinnamon is thought of as a good luck charm, and carrying a stick of it shields against malevolent energies.

Spatial Protection

Hang a bundle of cinnamon sticks above the entrance to protect the home from negative influences. Make your own room spray by infusing cinnamon and cloves in boiling water to create a homey and safe feel in your environment. You can dispel negativity by adding cinnamon sticks to hot water being used to wash floors or by burning sticks of it throughout the home.

Personal/Spiritual Growth

Cinnamon is a powerful healer, both physically and emotionally. It is the perfect spice for when you are feeling down or depressed. Use it in a sachet to raise protective and spiritual vibrations. Cinnamon brings good fortune in matters of money and business as well as games of chance—adding cinnamon oil to the outside of your purse or wallet is believed to attract both physical and spiritual prosperity. (See the Cinnamon entry in Chapter 4 to learn about the benefits of cinnamon essential oil.)

Clove

Description

Clove is an evergreen tree (*Syzygium aromaticum*) native to the Maluku Islands, an archipelago within Indonesia also called the Spice Islands. The flower bud of this tree is used in its dried form, either whole or ground—you may already have one or both in your spice cabinet. The word *clove* comes from the Latin *clavus*, meaning "nail." Take a look at a whole clove and you'll see why!

History and Lore

Archaeologists found cloves in a vessel in Syria that dates back to 1721 B.C.E. The ancient Chinese chewed cloves to freshen their breath. One of the world's oldest clove trees, estimated to have been between 350 and 400 years old, was one called Afo, located on the island of Ternate. In Indonesia, clove cigarettes, called kreteks, are extremely popular.

Uses

Healing Uses

Cloves can be used to treat toothaches, gum problems, and bad breath. Add cloves to tea to help clear up a respiratory infection. Eugenol, a natural antiseptic found in cloves, makes this spice useful for improving acne. Cloves are packed with antioxidants and are also effective for reducing heartburn, indigestion, and nausea. Clove is often used as a natural insect repellent. Use clove-infused water in a warm compress to soothe aching eyes.

Personal Protection

Clove is a very protective spice. It can be used to ward off negative forces, stop harmful gossip, and keep good friends close. Crush cloves into dust and sprinkle directly on you before walking into situations that feel socially precarious.

Spatial Protection

Burn cloves to cleanse and purify a space. They are especially helpful for use after an argument or negative situation. A pinch of cloves placed into a boiling pot of water is said to clear lingering adverse vibrations. Crushing cloves along with rosemary and carefully burning the powder is believed to foster a happy home environment.

Personal/Spiritual Growth

Clove dispels negativity and cleanses the aura. It rejuvenates physical and mental energy and fosters courage and inner strength. It can also be used for protection or to attract love. Infuse wine or apple cider with cloves to create a delicious aphrodisiac. Wear cloves in an amulet to stimulate the memory, and diffuse clove oil to assist in concentration. Drinking clove tea is a powerful way to amplify its benefits, helping you achieve clarity of mind and spiritual awareness. (See the Clove entry in Chapter 4 to learn about the benefits of clove essential oil.)

Comfrey

Description

The term *comfrey* is used to describe various perennial herbs of the genus *Symphytum*. It comes from the Latin *confervere*, meaning "to boil together." (The origin of the word *fervent* is also evident here—*fervere* meaning "to boil.") The most common variety is Russian comfrey, which has pink or purple flowers. Comfrey grows well in most temperate regions, including North America, Europe, western Asia, and Australia.

History and Lore

The ancient Greek physician, pharmacologist, and botanist Pedanius Dioscorides (c. 40–90) included comfrey in his writings about herbal medicine. Legend has it that comfrey was one of the herbs growing in the Garden of Eden. In the New World, the settlers relied on comfrey to treat various illnesses and conditions, and it was seen as particularly useful in the mending of broken bones. Comfrey in modern times is used topically, since it can have negative effects on the liver.

Uses

Healing Uses

Comfrey is excellent for treating wounds, particularly those that are dirty or have become infected (use a compress soaked with warm comfrey tea for this). Its ability to heal broken bones earned it the nickname "knitbone," and it also assists with strains, sprains, and torn ligaments. As a poultice, it relieves bruises and soreness. This herb also assists with coughs and other lung-related issues.

Personal Protection

Comfrey is used to protect travelers; place it in your luggage to prevent your bags from being stolen. Wrap your money in a comfrey leaf for several days before any gambling endeavors to increase your chances of winning. Burn comfrey to let go of an unhealthy relationship. It is also thought that giving a romantic partner a sachet of comfrey will protect the relationship and keep the person faithful during times apart.

Spatial Protection

Comfrey has a strong connection to the earth, making it a grounding force for emotional, physical, and even financial stability. Plant comfrey around your home to create a protective shield, invite wealth, and increase fertility. Placing comfrey leaves under your doormat is said to keep unwanted visitors away.

Personal/Spiritual Growth

Comfrey is a grounding herb that provides a sense of structure when things feel chaotic. It soothes emotional pain and provides comfort during difficult times. Comfrey is associated with the throat chakra, making it effective in using your voice to enforce boundaries, both physical and spiritual. Add this herb to bathwater after meditation or therapeutic work for spiritual cleansing.

Dandelion

Description

Known to most people as a common weed, dandelion (*Taraxacum officinale*) is a perennial plant belonging to the Asteraceae family. It features bright yellow flowers and is found worldwide. The leaves, flowers, and roots are all used for various medicinal and culinary purposes. The yellow flower heads mature and turn into feathery, white seed heads that then disperse in the wind, spreading the seeds far and wide. The word *dandelion* comes from the Latin *dens leonis*, meaning "lion's tooth," which refers to the shape of the plant's leaves.

History and Lore

Because dandelion flowers open early in the morning and close in the evening, the dandelion is sometimes called the "shepherd's clock." It is said that if the seeds fly off a dandelion seed head when there is no wind, it means rain is coming. The childhood act of blowing on a dandelion puff to make a wish or holding a bloom under your chin to look for the presence of a yellow glow (which could indicate a future fortune) dates back to medieval times.

Uses

Healing Uses

Dandelion is often used as a diuretic and to purify the cleansing organs. It contains taraxacin and choline, which stimulate liver cell metabolism. Dandelion flowers and stems can be eaten raw or cooked, as they are rich in vitamins A, B-complex, C, and E, as well as calcium. A tea made from dandelion roots is useful as a general health tonic. Rub the milky juice of the dandelion stem to heal warts.

Personal Protection

Dandelion leaves are helpful for protection from negative energies, particularly those coming from those who wish you harm. The puffballs can also be carried around with you as they can fortify your energy and bring luck.

Spatial Protection

Plant dandelions around your home and in your garden for protection and rejuvenation. It is a common misconception that these plants are invasive and unwanted weeds; in fact, they promote soil stability and attract pollinators.

Personal/Spiritual Growth

Dandelion stimulates the solar plexus chakra, the core of who we are. It helps to focus scattered emotions and strengthen the sense of self. This plant encourages those who are fearful of change to take action and move forward in life. Dandelions are powerful symbols of resilience and the ability to thrive in adversity. Blow on the white puffball of a dandelion seed head to check in with a relationship: If one seed remains after blowing on the seed head three times, it means your sweetheart is thinking of you. Then whisper a message to the flower and blow it in the direction of your loved one. Drink its tea to remove lingering unwanted energies that could hold back your growth. Drinking a tea of dandelion flowers increases psychic abilities. Pour boiling water over dandelion root for divination. Include dandelion in a dream pillow to ward off nightmares.

Echinacea

Description

Echinacea is a genus that includes several flowering plants in the daisy family. These coneflowers, as they're called, have pink or purple petals and are native to eastern and central North America. They typically bloom in midsummer and continue to flower until the first of winter. The word *echinacea* comes from the Latin *echinus*, meaning "sea urchin"—a reference to the plant's bristly seed head.

History and Lore

The Plains Native Americans used echinacea root as a painkiller and to treat colds, sore throats, wounds, and snakebites. The purple coneflower is still harvested by the Lakota people for medicinal uses. Echinacea was very popular in the United States in the eighteenth and nineteenth centuries, but its use declined after the introduction of antibiotics.

Uses

Healing Uses

Echinacea raises white blood cell count, stimulates the immune system, and has anti-carcinogenic, antibiotic, and anti-inflammatory properties. Chew on the root or drink as tea to fight infection or prevent colds and flu—or to decrease their duration if they have already taken hold. To relieve skin inflammation, burns, or insect bites, saturate a compress in echinacea tea and place on the affected area. Echinacea essential oil is very useful with massage. Rub it on the temples and the back of the neck to relieve tension in the head, neck, and shoulders. You can also add echinacea to most dishes as an edible garnish, or place its petals in ice cube trays to chill beverages while infusing them with its healing properties.

Personal Protection

Echinacea is a great addition to any herb satchel to ward off unwanted energies and provide protection on the go. It is highly regarded as a tool in mediumship, or communication with the dead. Adding it to channeling spaces, or drinking its tea before a session, is believed to facilitate and protect this interaction.

Spatial Protection

Echinacea grown around the house brings prosperity and protects the family from suffering, particularly in the financial sectors. Burn echinacea as incense to cleanse the home of unwanted energy, making sure to let the smoke waft freely throughout the space. It also can be added to your cleaning routine as a floor wash, further amplifying its benefits.

Personal/Spiritual Growth

Many spiritual and physical ailments are a result of denying who you really are. Echinacea awakens the true inner self and assists in integrating that self with the outside world. In addition, echinacea brings the mind and body into balance, creating a sense of inner harmony. This plant is also useful during major transitions, giving you strength and stamina in times of change.

Evening Primrose

Description

Evening primrose is a flowering plant of the Onagraceae family, which is native to the Americas. Its cup-shaped yellow flowers have four petals each and open in the evening (hence the name). The young roots and shoots can be eaten like a vegetable, and the whole plant can be used for medicinal and other purposes.

History and Lore

Many Native American tribes, including the Cherokee, Iroquois, and Ojibwa, used evening primrose for various rituals and remedies. They used it as a poultice to treat bruises, as a salve to relieve skin irritations, and as a tea for weight loss. Evening primrose root was also heated and applied to hemorrhoids to relieve pain and reduce swelling. The Shakers, a religious sect founded in England in the eighteenth century, used evening primrose in many of their natural remedies, including poultices for wounds and teas for upset stomach.

Uses

Healing Uses

Evening primrose is high in essential fatty acids that are necessary for good health. Women can take evening primrose oil as a nutritional supplement to ease symptoms of PMS or to boost fertility. The oil can also be used to calm skin issues such as eczema and rosacea by applying it to the affected area. A tea made from the leaves, stems, and roots, applied externally, is nourishing for the skin.

Personal Protection

Because it blooms at night, evening primrose is great for use in moon ceremonies. Evening primrose provides a protective shield during spiritual rituals. Add evening primrose to bathwater to enhance inner beauty or for good luck in your career. It is believed to ward off negative influences and can also be used to attract faeries; finding a patch of it is said to indicate a portal to the faerie realm nearby.

Spatial Protection

Place evening primrose flowers or leaves around your home to ward off negative energy and protect your space. Known for its soothing and healing qualities, evening primrose brings a sense of comfort to your home or office space. Hanging evening primrose plants on your porch or outdoor spaces will invite balance and restore harmony.

Personal/Spiritual Growth

As an evening bloomer, this flower shines its own light in the dark and encourages you to do the same. Evening primrose stimulates the solar plexus and heart chakras, allowing you to open yourself up to love without fear of betrayal or rejection. It also enhances creativity. Anointing candles, crystals, and yourself with evening primrose oil can amplify your intentions.

Fennel

Description

Fennel (*Foeniculum vulgare*) is a plant in the parsley and carrot family with small yellow flowers. Native to the Mediterranean region, this herb is very flavorful and aromatic. All parts of the plant, including the seeds, can be eaten, although the stalks are tough and not used as often. The white bulb and green fronds have a slightly sweet anise flavor.

History and Lore

Fennel has been used as a medicinal and culinary herb for thousands of years. In ancient Greece, athletes ate the seeds as a health food and to control their weight. The Romans had numerous medicinal uses for fennel, including the treatment of eye ailments. In the twelfth century, the German nun, writer, composer, philosopher, and mystic Saint Hildegard of Bingen (1098–1179) noted fennel's eye-healing properties.

Uses

Healing Uses

As a tea, fennel eases dizziness, coughs, and headaches. It can also be used as an expectorant to clear congestion. Fennel supports digestion and relieves abdominal cramps and flatulence, and it also increases milk flow in nursing mothers. The essential oil is especially useful during menstruation. Chewing fennel seeds freshens the breath.

Personal Protection

Fennel is associated with strength, courage, and protection, and it is particularly helpful in the face of danger. When feeling inundated by bad luck, burning a candle covered with ground fennel seeds will reboot your energy. Include fennel in sachets to remove negativity.

Spatial Protection

Burn fennel as incense to purify a space or to prevent ill intentions directed your way. Hang fennel over a doorway with Saint John's wort to ward off unwanted spiritual intrusion. Using the smoke from burned fennel seeds cleanses the energy of objects worked with during spiritual practice.

Personal/Spiritual Growth

Chewing fennel seeds right before a challenge brings immediate mental focus and allows for ideal expression. Sleeping with a sachet of fennel seeds, cinnamon, and rose is said to assist in attracting passion to your life. Fennel also improves relationships, assists in establishing boundaries, and helps others trust in your word. Fennel essential oil is excellent for grounding during meditation and other spiritual practices.

Garlic

Description

Native to central Asia, garlic (*Allium sativum*) is an onion-like plant with a bulb that separates into cloves. It has a strong flavor and odor; hence the nickname "stinking rose." Garlic grows worldwide, but China is the largest producer. The word *garlic* comes from the Old English *garleac*: *gar*, meaning "spear," and *leac*, meaning "leek."

History and Lore

The Romans used garlic to fend off evil spirits, and Greek soldiers carried it to prevent misfortune. In Romania, it was common practice to place garlic cloves in the mouths of the corpses of those thought to be vampires. Many traits of vampires, including their aversion to garlic, are also symptoms of a condition called porphyria, a rare metabolic disease characterized by large amounts of porphyrins in the blood and urine. (Garlic exacerbates the disease.)

Uses

Healing Uses

Garlic is used to improve digestion and ease stomach cramps. It also cleanses the blood, increases circulation, and can prevent heart attacks and strokes. You may make tea by crushing a clove of garlic in a cup of boiling water. Garlic bolsters the immune system and protects against and fights off illness, including the common cold and the flu. Garlic contains compounds that break down carcinogenic chemicals. Ingesting too much garlic can cause stomach inflammation, ulcers, and anemia.

Personal Protection

Garlic is a very protective plant. Its pungent aroma is ideal to repel negativity, evil, and the envy of others. Carrying it in your pocket is thought to ward off malevolent forces, and carrying it on trips across water is thought to protect against injury. Garlic oil can also be rubbed on the skin in lieu of holding the cloves.

Spatial Protection

Burning garlic cloves and dispersing the smoke around the home is said to clear dismal energy. Hang braided garlic above doorways to discourage unwanted visitors. Placing a clove of garlic in the four corners of the home creates a protective shield.

Personal/Spiritual Growth

Garlic assists with spiritual healing by removing negative energy and strengthening your inner self. It also fortifies willpower and helps you keep your sights on your goals, even when faced with obstacles. Additionally, garlic fights envy and jealousy in oneself and others. Consuming garlic is believed to amplify personal courage when taking on new fears and challenges.

Ginger

Description

Ginger (*Zingiber officinale*) is a tropical Southeast Asian plant with yellowish-green flowers and a pungent aromatic root. Gingerroot, as it is also called, is used either fresh or dried for both medicinal and culinary purposes. Because of its spicy flavor, this root is associated with energy and vigor.

History and Lore

Ginger has been featured in ancient Chinese medicine and Ayurveda for thousands of years. It was highly valued by the ancient Romans, but its use decreased dramatically after the fall of the Roman Empire. It was picked up again in Europe and in the sixteenth century was introduced to Africa and the Caribbean. Jamaican ginger was the first spice to be grown in the New World and exported back to Europe.

Uses

Healing Uses

Ginger has long been known as a stomach settler. It relieves nausea and vomiting associated with migraines, morning sickness, and motion sickness, and it is also helpful to those recovering from surgery or undergoing chemotherapy. Ginger treats the inflammation associated with arthritis, not only masking the pain but also fostering changes in the joints. Ginger is also a microbial herb that fights infectious illness. Incorporating ginger into foods and drinking it as a tea are the easiest ways to partake of its benefits.

Personal Protection

As an amulet, ginger enhances health and protection. Burn powdered ginger to immediately dispel unfavorable vibrations. Keeping a small piece of ginger root in your purse or pocket invites support and protection from the universe.

Spatial Protection

Burn dried ginger with palo santo to construct a highly effective energy cleanse for any space in your home. Hanging ginger around doorways shields the room from negative spiritual influences. Sprinkling powdered ginger around windows and doorways provides for an even more powerful deflection of malevolent forces.

Personal/Spiritual Growth

Ginger's digestive qualities extend into the spiritual realm. It helps you process ideas and emotions and provides the motivation needed to bring them into the physical realm. As an essential oil, ginger can bring energy and vitality. It is also a powerful aphrodisiac, corresponding to the sacral chakra, which governs pleasure. Ginger also makes spells work faster and helps plans develop more quickly. Writing your intention on a ginger root, and then burying it, speeds up the process of manifestation.

Ginseng

Description

Ginseng encompasses several species of plants of the genus *Panax* with forked roots and small greenish flowers grouped in umbels (flat or rounded clusters). The major varieties of ginseng include Asian (*Panax ginseng*) and American (*Panax quinquefolius*). Another major variety, Siberian ginseng (*Eleutherococcus senticosus*), is in the same family as the first two but of a different genus. The word *ginseng* comes from the Mandarin *renshen: ren*, meaning "person," and *shen*, meaning "root"—most likely due to the forked root shape's resemblance to human legs.

History and Lore

Ginseng has been used in China for 5,000 years. Because Chinese emperors treasured the plant, it became highly valued and in demand. Native Americans are responsible for ginseng's cultivation in North America. The Cherokee, Iroquois, and other tribes used ginseng as a remedy for various ailments and for general life enhancement.

Uses

Healing Uses

Ginseng is considered a panacea—a cure-all. It is an adaptogen, a natural substance that helps the body adapt to stress, and it also lowers blood sugar levels. Ginseng is associated with stimulation and virility. Drinking ginseng tonics and infusions is a popular way to receive the benefits of this plant. Those taking heart medications such as blood thinners should not take ginseng, as it could result in a negative interaction.

Personal Protection

Ginseng has long been used to protect and restore physical and spiritual energy. Burn ginseng root or powder as incense to repel negativity, drive away evil, and break unfavorable patterns. Drink ginseng tea before meditation to provide protection and enhance the spiritual connection.

Spatial Protection

Ginseng is said to align the energetic environment, as it detoxifies and promotes a sense of purpose. Burning ginseng root or incense rids any space of unwanted or stagnant energy. Displaying the image of ginseng roots artistically through the home or workspace encourages a peaceful and happy space.

Personal/Spiritual Growth

Ginseng boosts both mental and physical energy levels, which can then be used to harness internal power. It reduces psychological stress and sharpens mental powers. Ginseng also aids in visualization fulfillment. To manifest an intention, write it on a ginseng root and run it under fresh water. Take ginseng before meditation for enhanced clarity and a sense of calm. Ginseng is a powerful love herb. It generates passion and lust, especially when drunk as a tea. Carry ginseng root with you to attract love or money. As an amulet, it is believed to bring good fortune, prosperity, longevity, and fertility.

Hyssop

Description

Hyssop (*Hyssopus officinalis*) is a plant in the mint family with spikes of blue or purple flowers and aromatic leaves. The hyssop plant is of Eurasian origin but also grows in North America. Both the leaves and flowers of the hyssop plant are used for medicinal and other purposes, and hyssop oil is used as a flavoring and a fragrance. Beekeepers love hyssop, as it produces a rich, aromatic honey.

History and Lore

Though it is not identified by name, hyssop is believed to be one of the aromatic herbs mentioned in the Bible as a purification substance, particularly to cleanse the sinful. The herbs were dipped in water or vinegar and then waved like a wand over the afflicted persons, often lepers.

Uses

Healing Uses

Hyssop tea is effective as an expectorant or cough suppressant, and it can also be used to lessen digestive and intestinal problems, including gas and loss of appetite. It can be used to flavor meats, marinades, and other dishes. Adding hyssop to bathwater eases the pain associated with rheumatoid arthritis. As a salve, hyssop soothes bruises, insect bites, and bee stings. Hyssop essential oil can help prevent infection.

Personal Protection

Hyssop is a powerful herb that supports the third eye chakra, which governs insight and intuition. As an essential oil, it is known to calm the mind, purge negativity, and purify an energetic field. Anointing spiritual tools with hyssop provides purification, restoring a positive vibration.

Spatial Protection

In the home, hyssop protects against thieves and trespassers. Combined with other cleansing herbs like sage, it is useful for purifying a space to clear away unwanted energies. It can create a positive energy flow when planted in the garden. Hyssop is said to attract faeries and benevolent natural spirits while keeping less desirable entities away. Infusing water with hyssop and sprinkling it around the home can purify any space that feels negative or energetically unclean.

Personal/Spiritual Growth

This herb promotes spiritual opening. Add it to bathwater to cleanse the aura, or burn it to break bad patterns, disengage from negative attachments, and move forward in a positive way. Hyssop essential oil can be used in aromatherapy to calm an anxious mind and bring spiritual clarity and focus.

Lemongrass

Description

Lemongrass (*Cymbopogon citratus*) is an aromatic tropical Asian grass named for its citrusy smell and flavor. The stalks are used in cooking, and the fresh or dried leaves, and the essential oil derived from them, are used in medicine. Lemongrass oil is also used as a pesticide and a preservative.

History and Lore

Also known as "fever grass," lemongrass has been used to treat fever in India for hundreds of years. Ancient palm-leaf manuscripts found in India were preserved with lemongrass oil. Indigenous Australians used lemongrass as a drink and applied a lemongrass wash to sore eyes, cuts, and skin irritations. Lemongrass appears in many Asian traditional cuisines, including Thai and Vietnamese.

Uses

Healing Uses

Lemongrass has antibacterial and antifungal properties, as well as lots of antioxidants. To treat acne, place lemongrass in boiling water, remove from heat, and let the steam wash over the skin. It also has powerful pain-relieving properties, making it useful for headaches, stomachaches, joint pain, and muscle soreness (use the essential oil for these). Lemongrass tea alleviates coughs and soothes sore throats.

Personal Protection

Lemongrass is a powerful cleanser. It removes negativity and brings good luck, making it helpful for improving career, love, and family issues. When added to bathwater, lemongrass leaves have a purifying power. Using lemongrass oil can clear spiritual blockages.

Spatial Protection

The citrusy aroma of lemongrass invites positive energy while dispelling negativity. To clear unfavorable vibrations, add a few drops of lemongrass oil to your cleaner to use as a floor wash. Soaking bay leaves with lemongrass in a spray cleaner will clear out envy and stagnation. Burning a stick of lemongrass and dispersing its smoke will amplify its clearing powers.

Personal/Spiritual Growth

Lemongrass increases psychic powers and can be used for psychic cleansing and divination. Through its cleansing properties, lemongrass removes obstacles and assists in spiritual opening. It enriches communication and helps to make sense of confusing or frustrating situations, particularly with loved ones. As an essential oil, it brings a sense of calm and clarity and also fosters forgiveness—in ourselves and others. Added to bathwater, lemongrass boosts sexual energy. When used in aromatherapy, lemongrass reduces tension and stress and heightens the senses.

Marjoram

Description

Marjoram (*Origanum majorana*) is a perennial plant in the mint family with small purplish to white flowers and aromatic leaves. Also called sweet marjoram, this plant is native to the Mediterranean region. Its fresh and dried leaves are used for culinary and medicinal purposes. Oregano, a related herb, is sometimes called wild marjoram.

History and Lore

Marjoram was reportedly one of several herbs found in a 60,000-year-old Neanderthal grave, indicating that the use of this herb is as old as humanity itself. According to Roman mythology, the goddess of love, Venus, gave this plant its scent to remind mortals of her beauty. In Greek mythology, Venus's counterpart, Aphrodite, created marjoram and grew it on Mount Olympus. Aristotle claimed that tortoises ate marjoram after being bitten by snakes, and therefore recommended it as a cure for snakebite.

Uses

Healing Uses

As a tea, marjoram eases coughs, colds, and headaches. It also has sedative properties, which can help with insomnia and general tension and stress. Massaging with marjoram essential oil can soothe strains, sprains, and muscle aches. Apply a warm marjoram poultice to ease muscle cramps. Marjoram also boosts the immune system, aids digestion, and calms the stomach.

Personal Protection

Marjoram cleanses, purifies, and removes negativity. It is often included in wedding bouquets to protect the union and carried around daily to prevent psychic attacks. Be sure to replace the marjoram leaves regularly to ensure their protective potency.

Spatial Protection

Marjoram leaves scattered around the house can deflect bad luck, but be sure to replace them regularly. Grown in the garden, marjoram protects against malevolent forces. Lighting a marjoram-anointed candle promotes a feeling of peace and emotional balance.

Personal/Spiritual Growth

Marjoram is associated with the crown chakra, the area at the top of the head that governs our connection to the higher spiritual consciousness. Marjoram has a warming, calming quality, bringing peace to the mind, body, and spirit. It assists those who are grief-stricken by fostering acceptance and clearing the way for happiness. Scatter marjoram to attract a new lover, enhance a current romantic relationship, or release the grip of a love gone bad. When cooking with marjoram, incorporate it mindfully with loving intentions. Include marjoram in sachets to attract abundance. Place it under your pillow to bring revealing, meaningful dreams. Adding the herb to bathwater is a great way to process grief. Burning marjoram helps you move beyond the past, accept the changes in life, and look to the future.

Parsley

Description

Parsley (*Petroselinum crispum*) is a biennial Eurasian herb with edible leaves. Varieties include flat-leaf (Italian) parsley and curly-leaf parsley. The leaves have many culinary applications, while both the leaves and the roots are used in medicine. The word *parsley* comes from the Greek *petroselinon*: *petro*, meaning "rock," and *selinon*, meaning "celery."

History and Lore

The ancient Greeks associated parsley with death and used it in funeral ceremonies. One legend says that parsley is slow to germinate because the seed travels to the devil and back nine times before coming up, and any seeds that don't germinate were kept by the devil. Some people are superstitious about transplanting parsley, saying that it brings bad luck.

Uses

Healing Uses

Parsley is rich in vitamins C, A, and B as well as iron and calcium. It improves digestion and promotes cardiovascular health. A compress soaked in cooled parsley tea soothes puffiness and swelling. Apply a parsley poultice to insect bites. Parsley essential oil has antibacterial and antifungal properties and can be used to treat acne and skin infections. Parsley root can ease urinary and kidney conditions. Chewing on parsley cleans the teeth and freshens the breath. Parsley is sometimes used to bring on menstruation. Drinking parsley tea is thought to enhance fertility. Pregnant women should not eat large quantities of parsley.

Personal Protection

Parsley is said to amplify communication with the spiritual world, especially to protect and purify. Add a mesh bag of parsley to a purification bath by holding it under the running water. Placing parsley on the plate is thought to prevent food contamination.

Spatial Protection

Parsley is a protective herb, and one which when burned can be used to heighten psychic awareness. Sprinkling it around your home or office space creates a protective shield and clears mental clutter. Visiting a loved one's grave or memorial with a bouquet of parsley fosters connections beyond the physical realm.

Personal/Spiritual Growth

Parsley is an uplifting herb. It restores a sense of well-being and helps the user get out of a rut. Use parsley to increase strength and vitality following surgery or an illness. Parsley also encourages love and romance, bringing excitement to a relationship. Drink parsley tea to connect with its properties on a mindful level. Burn the dried herb as incense in rituals for the dead to honor them and process grief.

Peppermint

Description

Peppermint (*Mentha piperita*) is a cross between watermint and spearmint. This perennial plant has small purple or white flowers and aromatic leaves that are used for both culinary and medicinal purposes. Peppermint is native to Europe and the Middle East, but it is cultivated worldwide.

History and Lore

Greek mythology offers a creation story for peppermint: Hades, the god of the underworld, seduced a water nymph named Minthe and they entered into a relationship. When Hades's wife, Persephone, found out about the affair, she turned Minthe into a plant so that everyone would walk on her. Hades then gave the plant a pleasant scent, so that every time someone stepped on it they would be reminded of Minthe's beauty.

Uses

Healing Uses

Peppermint treats symptoms of cold and flu, particularly as an expectorant. It is also excellent for digestive issues such as bloating, cramping, diarrhea, nausea, and vomiting (this includes pregnancy-related discomfort). Peppermint contains menthol, a natural analgesic. This, along with selenium and zinc, makes it useful for reducing the redness and irritation associated with dandruff. Inhaling the scent of peppermint oil can relieve headaches.

Personal Protection

Peppermint is a protective herb. Its essential oil cleanses the spirit, increases spiritual attunement, and supports intuition. A few drops of it in a spray bottle also cleanses the aura. Peppermint essential oil brings alertness in the dream state and assists in remembering and learning from dreams. For this purpose, use it as an inhalation or include the leaves in a sachet placed underneath the pillow.

Spatial Protection

Rub the leaves on furniture or objects or burn dried leaves as incense in a new home to remove any negative energy. Sprinkle peppermint-infused water around the home to eliminate unfavorable energy and invite higher vibrations to enter. Diffuse peppermint oil to invigorate a workspace.

Personal/Spiritual Growth

Peppermint supports transformation, as it is a natural stimulant. It boosts energy and invigorates the mind, as well as increases awareness, perception, and sensitivity. Drinking peppermint tea invites passion, and can ease mental chatter, bringing clarity to your thoughts. You can also use peppermint to encourage prosperity. The essential oil is particularly useful when anointing oneself or spiritual tools (such as a candle) for overcoming resistance to change, as it eliminates fear of the unknown.

Raspberry

Description

Raspberry (*Rubus idaeus*) is a member of the rose family. Like a rose bush, this plant also has thorny stems. The edible fruit of the raspberry plant may be red, black, purple, or golden, depending on the variety. The leaves also have culinary and medicinal uses.

History and Lore

As hunter-gatherers, Paleolithic cave dwellers are known to have eaten raspberries. According to Greek mythology, Zeus's nursemaid, Ida, pricked her finger on a thorn of a raspberry bush and her blood dripped onto the fruit, changing it from white to red. Another version of the story says that the berries got their name when the gods found them growing on Mount Ida. (*Rubus idaeus* means "bramble bush of Ida.")

Uses

Healing Uses

Raspberry fruit and leaves are used in pregnancy to strengthen uterine tissue, assist with labor, and prevent hemorrhaging during and following birth. Due to its astringent properties, raspberry alleviates mouth sores, bleeding gums, and other oral inflammation. As a gargle, raspberry leaf soothes sore throats. The fresh or dried leaves can be used in a tea to relieve digestive problems and nausea. Raspberry seed oil benefits the skin. Raspberry leaf enhances sleep and brings good dreams.

Personal Protection

The raspberry plant is associated with fertility. The leaf and fruit can be dried and placed in an amulet to support the female reproductive organs or protect a pregnancy. Steeping the berries in wine and serving it to a lover protects a relationship and keeps it strong.

Spatial Protection

Planting a raspberry bush by a new business protects it while promoting vision and growth. Place raspberry brambles near doors or entryways to block unwanted energies, especially during the process of childbirth.

Personal/Spiritual Growth

First-year raspberry plants do not produce fruit but are essential to the future fertility of the plant. This is a reminder to be patient in creative endeavors, which may take time to fully reach their potential. Associated with the sacral chakra, the area that governs creativity, raspberry fosters personal ingenuity and emotional expression. The thorns of the plant remind us to be protective of the fruits of our labor.

Rosemary

Description

Native to the Mediterranean region, rosemary (*Rosmarinus officinalis*) is an aromatic evergreen shrub in the mint family with light bluish-purple flowers and grayish-green, needle-like leaves. The leaves and oil are used for both culinary and medicinal purposes.

History and Lore

Rosemary has long been associated with immortality, memory, and fidelity. The ancient Egyptians used rosemary in their embalming practices. The ancient Greeks and Romans placed rosemary sprigs in the hands of the dead and burned the herb as incense at funerals. Greek students wore rosemary sprigs in their hair to boost their memories. Rosemary was also incorporated into marriage and baptism ceremonies.

Uses

Healing Uses

Rosemary stimulates and strengthens the circulatory and nervous systems, and is used to ease anemia and low blood pressure. Used in a warm poultice, rosemary soothes sore muscles and joint pain. As a salve, rosemary relieves headaches, muscle aches, and swollen feet. Rosemary tea aids digestion. This herb can also be used as a natural insect repellent. Inhaling this herb is thought to reduce cortisol levels.

Personal Protection

Placing rosemary under the pillow assists with dream recall and banishes nightmares and unwanted dream visitations. Rosemary can also be used in purification and cleansing rituals.

Spatial Protection

Burn bunches of dried rosemary and sage to purify a space, ensuring that the smoke dispels evenly. Sachets of rosemary placed in front of the home invites good luck to enter. Diffuse rosemary oil to create a peaceful and relaxing home environment. Plant rosemary around the home to encourage positivity.

Personal/Spiritual Growth

Rosemary is a stimulating, purifying herb. It also attracts positive energy and facilitates remembrance. Add rosemary to bathwater to improve memory, or burn it during meditation or dream work to remember past lives, also to cleanse the spirit. Its memory-boosting properties make it a favorite among students and those whose work requires memorization. Drink rosemary tea to heighten cognitive function, boost alertness, and heighten vibration. (For information on the use of rosemary essential oil in aromatherapy, see the Rosemary entry in Chapter 4.)

Sage

Description

Sage (*Salvia officinalis*) is a perennial herb in the mint family with blue to purplish flowers and aromatic grayish-green leaves. Native to the Mediterranean region, sage has a long history of culinary and medicinal use. The word *sage* comes from the Latin *salvus*, meaning "healthy." A related herb, clary sage, is covered in Chapter 4 on essential oils.

History and Lore

According to Greek legend, Cadmus, the founder and first king of Thebes, discovered the medicinal properties of sage when the leaves were offered to him in a religious ceremony. In the Middle Ages, sage was used to treat fevers, liver disease, and epilepsy. It was once believed that young women could use sage in divination to see their future husbands. White sage (*Salvia apiana*), which differs from the sage used commonly for culinary purposes, is native to the southwestern US and is used primarily in ceremonial purification.

Uses

Healing Uses

Sage improves many common mouth and throat ailments, including inflamed gums, laryngitis, and tonsillitis. Chewing the leaves cleans the teeth and freshens breath. For sore throats, gargle with sage tea. As a hair wash, sage helps eliminate head lice. Sage's antiseptic qualities make it useful as a compress or salve for treating wounds. As a facial steam bath, sage acts as an astringent for the skin and relieves congestion associated with head colds.

Personal Protection

Lighting sage releases its properties of purification, removing residual negative energies from your person. Hold and light a bundle of sage while setting an intention to release as it burns. Its scent allows for emotional healing and assists in letting go of past pain. You can make your own sage spray or carry its dried leaves in a pouch for an on-the-go way to cleanse and protect your energy.

Spatial Protection

Sage is used to cleanse a person, object, or space of negative energies or influences. This process, also called "saging," involves burning a bundle of dried sage leaves and letting the smoke waft over the person, object, or space. The smoke attaches to the negative energy and carries it away (be sure to keep windows open when saging to allow smoke to escape).

Personal/Spiritual Growth

Sage is a powerful herb, cleansing both the body and mind of impurities. Burn sage as incense to reestablish physical, spiritual, or emotional balance or to de-stress and relieve anxiety. Use sage oil or smoke in meditation to increase clarity and strengthen the connection to higher consciousness. If using white sage for spiritual connection, ensure it has been ethically harvested. White sage is sacred to many Native American tribes and is endangered due to overharvesting. In aromatherapy, sage essential oil stimulates the mind and relieves mental fatigue and depression.

Saint John's Wort

Description

Native to Europe and western Asia, Saint John's wort (*Hypericum perforatum*) is a shrubby perennial with bright yellow flowers. When rubbed, the flowers and leaves yield a red oil that has many medicinal uses. This herb gets its name from its connection to Saint John's Day, celebrated in late June. The word *wort* comes from the Old English *wyrt*, meaning "plant."

History and Lore

Originally a pagan celebration centered on the summer solstice, Saint John's Day, also known as Midsummer, is also a major religious holiday. Depending on the cultural tradition, it may be celebrated any day between June 21 and 25. Christians designated June 24 as the feast day of Saint John the Baptist, but observance begins the day before, known as Saint John's Eve. In medieval Europe, wreaths of Saint John's wort were worn on this holiday and then thrown into bonfires to ensure a plentiful harvest. The herb was also thought to protect against witchcraft.

Uses

Healing Uses

The most common medicinal use of Saint John's wort is to help relieve depression, but it is also used for anxiety, insomnia, and headaches, particularly migraines. An ointment made from the leaves and flowers relieves swelling, muscle cramps, and rheumatism. As a tea, Saint John's wort eases the symptoms of menopause.

Personal Protection

This protective herb has long been used as a symbol of lightness defeating the dark and can be burned to banish negative influences or used in purification rituals for spiritual cleansing. Place it under the pillow or use its oil for romantic, prophetic dreams. Wearing its dried leaves in an amulet provides protection from unwanted spiritual influences.

Spatial Protection

Saint John's wort safeguards spaces, and can be hung over doorways to repel negativity and provide spiritual protection. Create a wreath with Saint John's wort to attract prosperity and aid in all manner of well-being. Decorating your mantel with this herb amplifies its ability to dispel negativity from your space and produce abundance. Adding its leaves to a bonfire creates a shield of protection while inviting positivity to enter.

Personal/Spiritual Growth

Saint John's wort brings light in times of darkness and acts as a calming influence. As a flower essence, it stimulates the solar plexus chakra, helping those who feel vulnerable and fearful to find their inner power. Drink its tea to connect with focus to your spiritual journey. Carry Saint John's wort on your person to strengthen your convictions, especially when dealing with confrontations.

Valerian

Description

Valerian (*Valeriana officinalis*) is a perennial flowering plant native to Eurasia. Its fragrant pink or white flowers are used for flower extracts, and its roots (considered to be rather foul-smelling) are used for various medicinal purposes. This plant's name comes from the Latin word *valere*, meaning "to be strong or healthy."

History and Lore

The Greek physician Pedanius Dioscorides recommended the use of valerian to treat urinary tract infections and as an antidote to poisons. Legend has it that the fabled Pied Piper used valerian root along with his magic flute to lure rats away from the town of Hamelin, Germany, during the Middle Ages. Valerian was used to treat shell shock in soldiers during World War I.

Uses

Healing Uses

Valerian has a tranquilizing and sedative effect on the nervous system, making it excellent for reducing insomnia, anxiety, and headaches. It is especially soothing when drunk as a tea or added to bathwater. Valerian relaxes the muscles of the gastrointestinal tract and has been used to relieve cramping, diarrhea or constipation, gas, and irritable bowel syndrome. Note that excessive or prolonged use of valerian may be habit-forming.

Personal Protection

Its pungent odor is a deterrent to malevolent energy. Keep a satchel nearby in meditation to shield yourself while you spiritually connect. Used in bathwater, valerian provides protection from negative influences. Valerian assists with the connection to the subconscious. Include valerian in a dream pillow to ward off nightmares. It induces lucid dreaming and prophetic visions. As an amulet, valerian provides protection from unfavorable forces directed at you.

Spatial Protection

Sprinkle powdered valerian root at the front door to deter unwanted visitors. To maintain harmony in your space, mix valerian with a blend of rosemary, sage, and salt and spread it around the perimeter of your home. Burn valerian to cleanse and purify a space.

Personal/Spiritual Growth

In this area, valerian flower essence (see Chapter 3 for more on flower essences) is more effective than the root. Unresolved anger and negative emotions can lead to issues including headaches, anxiety, and high blood pressure. Use valerian flower essence in aromatherapy practices to unearth these buried feelings of guilt, anger, and negativity and replace them with self-love and acceptance. Valerian also helps you see the positive side of seemingly negative situations.

Yarrow

Description

Native to Eurasia, yarrow (*Achillea millefolium*), also known as milfoil, is an aromatic perennial with small, feathery leaves and clusters of small white flowers. The whole plant is used in herbal medicine. The genus *Achillea* gets its name from the Greek hero Achilles, and the species name (*millefolium*) means "thousand leaf."

History and Lore

According to Greek mythology, the great warrior Achilles used yarrow to treat the wounds of his fellow soldiers during the Trojan War. Yarrow is used in the ancient Chinese system of I Ching divination. It is said that yarrow grows on the grave of the Chinese philosopher Confucius (551–479 B.C.E.) in the Kong Lin Cemetery in China's Shandong province. During the American Civil War, yarrow was used as a surgical dressing to stanch blood flow.

Uses

Healing Uses

Yarrow stanches both internal and external bleeding. It is also a common remedy for colds and flu, and it helps to break fevers by promoting perspiration. As a poultice, yarrow helps manage infections and swelling. Inhaling the steam from yarrow tea calms allergies and aids respiratory problems such as asthma. Applied topically, yarrow essential oil supports wound healing; in aromatherapy it relieves stress and tension.

Personal Protection

The protective and healing power of yarrow extends to the personal and spiritual realms. Yarrow is especially helpful for highly sensitive people; carrying it offers protection from emotional absorption while doing healing or therapeutic work for others. Burning yarrow cleanses the aura.

Spatial Protection

Sprinkle dried yarrow flowers to cleanse any space and keep negative energies at bay. This is especially helpful for newly married couples. It is said that hanging yarrow flowers above the bridal bed ensures that the marriage will last at least seven years. Strewn across the threshold, yarrow protects the home from evil. Plant yarrow in your garden to enhance the powers of other plants and herbs, as well as to provide good energy to your outdoor space.

Personal/Spiritual Growth

Yarrow assists with all forms of psychic connection. Drink yarrow tea before divination to help focus the mind and avoid distractions. Yarrow also brings courage, clarity, and strength and aids in decision-making. Drink the tea or carry a piece of yarrow with you to enjoy these benefits. You may also inhale its oil rubbed between your hands for a quick boost of courage on the go.

3

The Power of Flower Essences

Nature provides subtle yet powerful remedies in the form of flower essences. Flower essences are infusions made from the flowering parts of plants that can support the emotional and mental aspects of your wellness. They are thought to hold both the energetic imprint of the flower's healing qualities and the earthly wisdom of the flower itself. They differ from essential oils and herbal tinctures in that they do not possess any physical part of the flower itself within. Often they have no scent and are in liquid form. These can be tools for soulful healing and spiritual transformation, as they are vibrational medicines that assist in the alignment of your inner peace.

Although flower essences have been used in countless cultures all over the world, perhaps the most famous practitioner of modern flower essences was Dr. Edward Bach (1886–1936). Bach was a British physician, homeopath, bacteriologist, and writer best known for developing a form of alternative medicine called Bach flower remedies. While he studied the various physical causes of disease, he felt there was also an unseen emotional component to human health. He began to experiment with plants and how they made him feel, and then developed theories about the powers of each one. Bach believed that when early morning sunlight shone on a plant, the light transferred the plant's power to the dewdrops that had collected on its flower petals during the night. He began collecting the dew but soon discovered it did not create a large enough yield. This led him to soak flowers in spring water and place the infusions in sunlight. Thus, Bach flower remedies were born. This chapter contains quotations from Bach's *The Twelve Healers and Other Remedies*.

Many companies sell Bach's thirty-eight original flower remedies, along with other flower essences and related products. You can also make your own: Essences are made by placing flowers in water and leaving them in the sunlight for hours. This process infuses the life force and healing power of the flower into the water. The essences are then often preserved with alcohol and diluted into a bottle for preservation.

Flower essences usually come in small dropper bottles and are meant to be taken orally, either on their own or mixed into a beverage. Additionally, you may even use them in a room spray. Follow the instructions on the bottle for best results.

Borage

Description

Native to the Mediterranean region, borage (*Borago officinalis*), also known as starflower, is an annual herb with blue or white star-shaped flowers and bristly stems and leaves. The whole plant is edible, but the flowers in particular are favored for their cucumber-like taste, which makes borage flower essence cool and refreshing. It is believed the word *borage* comes from the Arabic *abu araq*, meaning "source of sweat"—due to its use as a sudorific (a substance that cools the body by stimulating the sweat glands).

History and Lore

The Roman naturalist and philosopher Pliny the Elder (23–79) wrote that borage "maketh a man merry and joyful." Borage is also believed to be the herb called nepenthe in Homer's *Odyssey*—a drug that is supposed to help one forget one's sorrow. Borage flowers steeped in wine was a medieval cure for melancholy.

Uses

Borage flower essence is known first and foremost as a courage enhancer, helping you find the inner strength you need to overcome obstacles in life. It brings light and clarity during dark times. Borage also soothes the heavyhearted by opening the heart chakra; helping to release the emotions that cause depression; and making way for optimism, enthusiasm, and joy. It alleviates sorrow, and is helpful for overcoming discouragement. Borage essence is valuable for helping you extend compassion to a large group of people or a community, so you can spray borage before a stressful meeting or large social gathering. When you need a dose of encouragement and empathy, this essence provides both.

Cherry Plum

Description

Cherry plum (*Prunus cerasifera*) is a deciduous shrub in the rose family with white or pale pink flowers and small red or yellow fruit. Both the flowers and the fruit have culinary and medicinal uses, and it is also a popular ornamental shrub. Cherry plum is one of Bach's original flower remedies.

History and Lore

Not much is known about the history of cherry plum. It is believed to have originated in Asia, and it is now cultivated in Europe and North America as well. Cherry plums are a key ingredient in Georgian cuisine such as tkemali sauce, kharcho soup, and chakapuli stew. Bach categorized cherry plum under remedies for fear: "fear of the mind being over-strained, of reason giving way, of doing fearful and dreaded things, not wished and known wrong, yet there comes the thought and impulse to do them." This kind of fear can consume your life, causing anxiety, damaging personal relationships, and even jeopardizing your career.

Uses

This flower essence helps those who live in fear of losing control, by providing access to a person's deep personal reservoirs of inner strength and wisdom. Once in touch with these inner resources, the fearful person can find a way out of the cycle and loosen the grip that fear has on their life. Cherry plum essence assists with spiritual surrender and trust, allowing you to accept guidance by higher consciousness and powers. It also increases patience and decreases overwhelm. It's particularly helpful for busy parents and those in hectic management positions, encouraging clarity in the chaos.

Clematis

Description

Mainly of Japanese or Chinese origin, *Clematis* is a genus of about three hundred species of climbing plants in the buttercup family with flowers or fruit clusters. The name comes from the Greek *klematis*, meaning "climbing plant or vine." Clematis is one of Bach's original flower remedies.

History and Lore

Native Americans used clematis as a remedy for migraines, nervous disorders, and skin infections. Early American settlers used clematis as a pepper substitute to spice up food since real pepper was expensive and difficult to obtain. Bach categorized clematis as a solution when there is "not sufficient interest in present circumstances." He wrote that this flower essence is useful for "those who are dreamy, drowsy, not fully awake, no great interest in life. Quiet people, not really happy in their present circumstances, living more in the future than in the present; living in hopes of happier times, when their ideals may come true. In illness some make little or no effort to get well, and in certain cases may even look forward to death, in the hope of better times; or maybe, meeting again some beloved one whom they have lost."

Uses

This flower essence brings you back down to earth and into the present so you can live a better life. It is helpful for promoting focus and attention. It is particularly valuable for those working in the spiritual domains and creatives, as it supports balance of the physical and ethereal realms. It also is beneficial for grounding and creating a feeling of being fully present in the physical body. Clematis has been used for physical symptoms as well, such as when feeling a lack of energy or experiencing cold hands and feet due to poor circulation. Use clematis when switching gears from a creative or spiritual endeavor to a more everyday task because it will assist with the transition.

Crab Apple

Description

Malus is a genus of thirty to fifty species of deciduous trees or shrubs that includes the domesticated orchard apple. Native to North America and Eurasia, these trees have clusters of white, pink, or reddish flowers and produce small, tart fruit sometimes used in culinary preparations such as jelly or preserves. Crab apple is one of Bach's original flower remedies.

History and Lore

The origin of the term *crab apple* is unknown. Theories include the taste of the fruit, which is considered sour and disagreeable (like a crabby person), and the crooked shape of the tree's branches resembling a crab's legs. Some also suggest that it comes from a Norse word meaning "fruit of the wild apple tree."

Bach categorized it under "for despondency or despair." He wrote: "This is the remedy of cleansing. For those who feel as if they have something not quite clean about themselves. Often it is something of apparently little importance; in others there may be more serious disease which is almost disregarded compared to the one thing on which they concentrate. In both types they are anxious to be free from the one particular thing which is greatest in their minds and which seems so essential to them that it should be cured. They become despondent if treatment fails. Being a cleanser, this remedy purifies wounds if the patient has reason to believe that some poison has entered which must be drawn out."

Uses

Crab apple essence can help people who feel negative about their appearance, personality, or self-image. It calms the obsession with finding fault and can reduce negative self-talk. Crab apple essence is supportive to perfectionists and those in adolescence, as it assists with letting go of self-critique and raising confidence. It is particularly helpful as a room spray in the spaces you get ready in, as it assists with self-image. Place drops in a room spray or add a few drops to food and beverages.

Dandelion

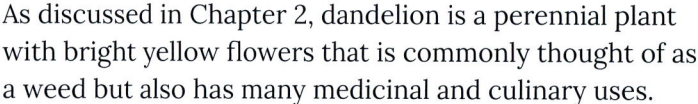

Description

As discussed in Chapter 2, dandelion is a perennial plant with bright yellow flowers that is commonly thought of as a weed but also has many medicinal and culinary uses.

History and Lore

See the Dandelion entry in Chapter 2.

Uses

Dandelion flower essence connects with the solar plexus chakra, where issues related to fear, anger, and self-worth are stored. It helps you release negative feelings toward yourself and others, and battles addictive and compulsive behaviors and thoughts. This flower essence assists those who feel like they are caught in a cycle and therefore can't enjoy the natural flow of life. It can help you listen closely to your own personal needs and live in a more effortless, natural way.

Just as its roots reach deep into the ground, almost impossible to pull out, while its light head blows its seeds into the wind with little resistance, the dandelion invites you to stay grounded while living lightly as a spiritual being. Dandelion flower essence also supports your inner power and the ability to stay present in your daily life. It is restorative to emotional stability and mental health, and amplifies your existing resources of self. This essence can quiet busy minds and help with recognizing and expressing feelings. Take dandelion flower essence when you feel overwhelmed about a decision or need to take a break from burdensome thoughts. It works well on its own, applied as drops on the tongue a few times a day.

Forget-Me-Not

Description

Forget-me-nots include a number of species of flowering plants of the genus *Myosotis*. The plant's name is borrowed from the German *Vergissmeinnicht*, and its small blue flowers have many uses in herbal medicine.

History and Lore

According to legend, during medieval times, a knight was walking next to a river with his beloved and bent down to pick flowers for her. He lost his balance and fell into the river, and his heavy armor started to drag him under. Before drowning, he tossed the flowers up to his lady and shouted, "Forget me not!" As a result, it is believed that those who wear this flower will never be forgotten by their lovers.

Uses

Forget-me-not flower essence calms and comforts by bringing you into contact with the larger spiritual world and connecting you to other levels of consciousness. As a result, it enhances personal relationships. In some cases, it may even restore a connection to a lost loved one. This flower essence offers guidance and a sense of purpose, as well as a feeling that everything is connected. This support can make a significant impact if you are feeling lost and alone.

Forget-me-not also provides mental clarity and stimulates information recall, making it a great essence to take in emergency situations and sudden life challenges. This essence releases negative thought patterns and is supportive for a restful night's sleep. It's also very useful in meditation, since it increases connection between the crown chakra and the conscious mind. When missing a loved one who has crossed over, forget-me-not essence can provide a comforting feeling of connection.

Gentian

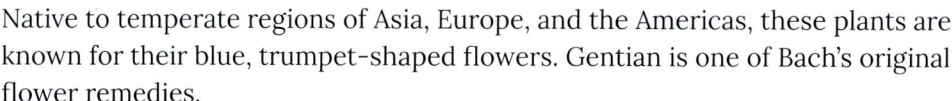

Description

Gentiana is a large genus of flowering plants with about four hundred species.
Native to temperate regions of Asia, Europe, and the Americas, these plants are known for their blue, trumpet-shaped flowers. Gentian is one of Bach's original flower remedies.

History and Lore

Gentian most likely gets its name from Gentius, an Illyrian king who ruled during the second century B.C.E. and who may have been the first to discover the plant's medicinal properties. According to legend, in the eleventh century, the Hungarian king Ladislaus prayed for divine help with a disease that was afflicting his subjects. He then shot an arrow into the air, and when he found it, it was embedded in a gentian root, which proved to be the remedy needed to cure the disease.

Bach categorized gentian under "for those who suffer uncertainty" and recommended the flower essence for "those who are easily discouraged. They may be progressing well in illness or in the affairs of their daily life, but any small delay or hindrance to progress causes doubt and soon disheartens them."

Uses

Gentian essence lifts downhearted feelings and speeds up the process of bouncing back from setbacks. Gentian essence is also supportive for reinstating an uplifting mood, as it can open the mind to encouragement and a positive outlook. When feeling inundated with setbacks, in over your head, or like a failure, using gentian will nudge your mood to a state of renewed conviction. For example, this essence can be of use to those on a hunt for a new job or students who are struggling with self-confidence after poor performance on a test. For the physical body, gentian is known for its ability to relieve muscular cramps. It is also believed to be helpful with a variety of digestive issues as well as liver dysfunction and overall fatigue.

Gorse

Description

Gorse is any of the flowering plants of the genus *Ulex*, which comprises about twenty species of thorny evergreen shrubs. Native to Europe, these plants have fragrant, edible yellow flowers and black pods. Gorse is one of Bach's original flower remedies.

History and Lore

Gorse was brought to New Zealand in the 1830s, and it rapidly took over areas of cleared land and farmland. Over time it became known as an invasive weed, and great sums of money have been spent on controlling its spread. It is estimated that gorse covers between 3 and 5 percent of New Zealand's total land area.

Bach said gorse was well suited "for those who suffer uncertainty" and he recommended the flower essence for those suffering from "very great hopelessness, they have given up belief that more can be done for them. Under persuasion or to please others they may try different treatments, at the same time assuring those around that there is so little hope of relief."

Uses

Gorse flower essence shines a light on the path out of despair, restoring faith and helping you move forward. Gorse essence is beneficial to those feeling hopeless in the face of a challenging life situation or plagued with a pessimistic mindset. This essence promotes hope, happiness, and resilience. It eases apathy and allows a cheerful attitude toward life. This essence is particularly helpful for facing chronic health conditions or a daunting diagnosis, and for those supporting someone in that situation. Gorse essence is a remedy for hopelessness as it opens your eyes to the light that exists even in the midst of darkness. Try gorse essence when you're ready for a new outlook on life and your purpose within it.

Honeysuckle

Description

Honeysuckle is a shrub or vine belonging to the genus *Lonicera* with fragrant, tubular flowers and small berries. The genus gets its name from the German botanist Adam Lonicer (1528–1586). Honeysuckle is one of Bach's original flower remedies.

History and Lore

There are many varieties of honeysuckle, including Japanese honeysuckle, orange honeysuckle, and coral honeysuckle. Japanese honeysuckle was introduced to the United States in the early to mid-1800s for ornamental use and as a soil stabilizer. Orange honeysuckle attracts hummingbirds. Native Americans smoked the dried leaves of coral honeysuckle to relieve the symptoms of asthma.

Bach found that honeysuckle helped people with "not sufficient interest in present circumstances." He recommended this flower essence for "those who live much in the past, perhaps a time of great happiness, or memories of a lost friend, or ambitions which have not come true. They do not expect further happiness such as they have had."

Uses

Honeysuckle essence helps you learn from rather than live in the past, showing you that there is much to look forward to. This is also good for homesickness and nostalgia. It encourages you to stay in the present moment and move through life without being held back by regrets of yesterday. When looking back into the past, honeysuckle can help you use a lens of reflection, gratitude, and appreciation, rather than disdain and pain. It is especially helpful when in the midst of changing homes or when working to let go of a past mistake or regret. For physical health, it is known to soothe skin irritations and improve skin texture and tone. As a room spray, it creates a calming and peaceful environment. Honeysuckle essence room spray makes a great gift for university students moving away from home for the first time.

Impatiens

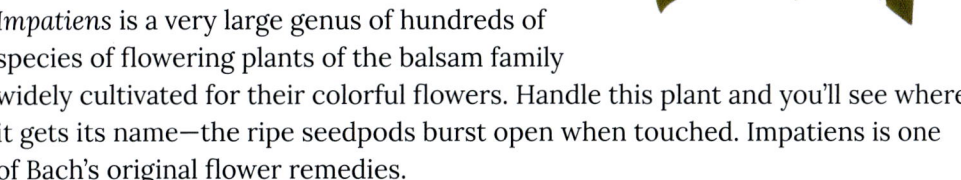

Description

Impatiens is a very large genus of hundreds of species of flowering plants of the balsam family widely cultivated for their colorful flowers. Handle this plant and you'll see where it gets its name—the ripe seedpods burst open when touched. Impatiens is one of Bach's original flower remedies.

History and Lore

Impatiens were discovered growing in eastern Africa and are believed to have originated in Zanzibar, an island off the coast of present-day Tanzania. The British physician and naturalist John Kirk introduced impatiens to the Western world in 1896. Bach categorized impatiens under "loneliness" and wrote that this flower essence is helpful to "those who are quick in thought and action and who wish all things to be done without hesitation or delay. When ill they are anxious for a hasty recovery. They find it very difficult to be patient with people who are slow as they consider it wrong and a waste of time, and they will endeavor to make such people quicker in all ways. They often prefer to work and think alone, so that they can do everything at their own speed."

Uses

Impatiens essence can help you relax, slow down, and understand that things take time. It also encourages you to be more accepting when dealing with others. This essence can be considered the equivalent of taking a deep breath to calm down, and proves valuable to those who struggle completing tasks they begin. It calms irritability in handling situations that are not in our control. It is exceptionally helpful for parents, leaders, and managers because it enhances self-confidence and reduces procrastination. Finally, it aids in keeping a calm demeanor after being dealt an emotional blow and supports a feeling of being in control. Spray impatiens essence in a room when dealing with angry customers or toddlers having tantrums.

Lily

Description

Lily is a plant of the genus *Lilium* that grows from a bulb and has large, often trumpet-shaped flowers. The flowers can be a variety of colors and are usually fragrant. Alpine lily, calla lily, Easter lily, and mariposa lily are just a few of the many varieties of this plant.

History and Lore

According to biblical lore, lilies were found growing in Gethsemane after Christ died—the garden where Jesus prayed and the apostles slept the night before the crucifixion. In ancient Greece, the lily was associated with Hera, the goddess of marriage. Lily is often featured in art and literature as a symbol for purity and innocence. In China, several lily species are cultivated as root vegetables. Lily root is also featured in Japanese cuisine, especially as an ingredient in chawan-mushi, a savory egg custard.

Uses

Lily flower essence is a supportive addition to the bath and spaces of self-care, either as a room spray or salve. Lily essence is especially beneficial when dealing with a lack of connection to the female self. Alpine lily flower essence helps women integrate all sides of their feminine identities and stay grounded in their bodies. Calla lily flower essence expands the notion of sexual identity and is best taken with a partner. Easter lily flower essence manages the tension between sexuality and spirituality. Mariposa lily flower essence enables people to act as mothers to themselves, healing feelings of separation and alienation and bringing comfort, joy, and freedom. Lily essence provides a foundation for self-assurance and refortifies physical presence in the female body.

Red Clover

Description

Red clover (*Trifolium pratense*) is a Eurasian perennial with rose-colored flowers and trifoliate leaves (hence the genus name). It is largely used as a cover crop, to protect and enrich the soil, and is also a favorite of grazing farm animals. The idiom "in clover" describes a carefree life of ease, comfort, and prosperity.

History and Lore

In ancient China, dried red clover was burned at altars as incense. Medieval Christians associated this plant's three-part leaves with the holy trinity. There is a long history of red clover being used to treat cancer, specifically breast, ovarian, and lymphatic cancers. Red clover became the state flower of Vermont in 1895. The flower of the red clover is actually many tiny flowers clustered together. Its unique shape appears flame-like, and its ancient alchemical symbol is the chevron, which relates to forces of fire and air. In Scandinavia the chevron is called a *sparre*, resembling the English word *spear*.

Uses

When your sense of identity feels tenuous or threatened, red clover flower essence keeps you firmly rooted in your beliefs, making it especially helpful in times of chaotic events on a worldwide scale. It supports self-awareness and helps you locate and act from your own center of truth. This flower essence also encourages a calm demeanor in crisis situations. It transforms lower-frequency emotional states like fear or panic into expanded states of consciousness. Keep red clover essence to spray in meeting rooms or any space where conversations can become contentious. Red clover essence is also helpful when cleansing or balancing is needed.

Rose

Description

The genus *Rosa* comprises many species of shrubs and vines with prickly stems and fragrant flowers. Most species are native to Asia, although some are native to Europe, North America, and northwestern Africa. The Latin *rosa* might derive from the Greek *Rhodia*, meaning "originating from Rhodes," a Greek city. Rock rose and wild rose are two of Bach's original flower remedies.

History and Lore

Ornamental roses were cultivated in the Mediterranean, Persia, and China as early as 500 B.C.E. The French empress Joséphine de Beauharnais (1763–1814) adored roses and maintained a famous rose garden at her Château de Malmaison. Prior to her marriage to Napoleon, she was known by the name Rose.

Bach categorized the variety called rock rose under "for those who have fear" and recommended the flower essence as "the remedy of emergency for cases where there even appears no hope. In accident or sudden illness, or when the patient is very frightened or terrified, or if the condition is serious enough to cause great fear to those around. If the patient is not conscious the lips may be moistened with the remedy." He said wild rose was helpful for people with "not sufficient interest in present circumstances" and recommended the flower essence to "those who without apparently sufficient reason become resigned to all that happens, and just glide through life, take it as it is, without any effort to improve things and find some joy. They have surrendered to the struggle of life without complaint."

Uses

Rose essence is beneficial to the heart chakra, in that it supports letting go all that is not of a loving nature within. It inspires a perspective of heart-centered thinking, serenity, and connection to unconditional love. If you are feeling separated from your inner self, rose essence can help you reconnect to your spiritual consciousness. Drink tea with rose essence or incorporate it into your nighttime skin care routine to assist with your emotional balance.

Star of Bethlehem

Description

Star of Bethlehem may be any of the plants of the genus *Ornithogalum*, which grow from a bulb and have star-shaped white flowers. Some of the plants of this genus are edible and eaten as vegetables, while others are poisonous. Native to the Mediterranean region, star of Bethlehem is one of Bach's original flower remedies.

History and Lore

This plant is named for the star that guided the magi to Bethlehem to see the baby Jesus. Because of its biblical name, it has come to be associated with purity, hope, love, and happiness. It is also a popular choice for religious ceremonies, weddings, and romantic gestures.

   This is the flower essence for those unexpected, unfortunate events in life. Bach found that star of Bethlehem was useful "for despondency or despair" and suggested it "for those in great distress under conditions which for a time produce great unhappiness. The shock of serious news, the loss of someone dear, the fright following an accident, and such like. For those who for a time refuse to be consoled, this remedy brings comfort."

Uses

Trauma can have long-lasting negative effects on the mind, body, and spirit. Star of Bethlehem flower essence uncovers unresolved issues resulting from trauma so that they can be dealt with before they begin to manifest in other harmful ways. This essence is extremely helpful for those grieving the death of a loved one or enduring a negative life-altering experience. Have star of Bethlehem on hand for use when dealing with the shock of unwelcome news. It provides comfort to those who are despondent and withdrawn while it supports emotional healing.

Sunflower

Description

The genus *Helianthus* comprises about seventy species of sunflowers, most of which are native to North America; a few are native to South America. This tall plant has a large, round, yellow flower head with petals reminiscent of the rays of the sun. The name comes from the Greek: *helios* ("sun") plus *anthos* ("flower").

History and Lore

Evidence suggests that Native Americans cultivated sunflowers in present-day Arizona and New Mexico as early as 3000 B.C.E., perhaps even before corn. They ate the seeds, ground them to make flour, and extracted oil from them. The Incas of South America treasured the flower for its resemblance to the sun and associated it with Inti, the sun god. The Spanish brought sunflowers to Europe in the 1500s.

Uses

Much like the sun radiates from the sky, your soul radiates from your inner self. Sunflower flower essence harnesses your inner radiance and lets it shine outward. It helps to balance the crown chakra, which controls mental energy and is your connection to the divine. Sunflower essence is beneficial for any stage of life in which the authentic self is feeling lackluster or darkened by the limitations of negative personal beliefs. Take sunflower essence when feeling self-critical, or spray it in a room to lift the spirits of those who seem sullen or downtrodden. It also fosters courage and self-confidence in those of us who mask our true selves hoping for love and acceptance. This flower essence celebrates each of us as a unique individual.

4

The Power of Essential Oils

The use of aromatic plants and oils for healing, beauty, and vitality is an ancient practice that is so powerful that it continues even today. Essential oils are liquids that are extracted from aromatic plants and then used for healing and therapeutic practices. They are powerful, highly concentrated substances, and most have to be diluted in a carrier oil (such as sweet almond, jojoba, or grape-seed) before use. These fragrant oils are what draw bees to flowers and cause you to stop and, quite literally, smell the roses. The ancient Egyptians, Greeks, and Romans were the first to use aromatic plant oils in baths and massage for healing and therapeutic purposes, and these practices are still widely used in modern aromatherapy. (Aromatherapy is further explored in Chapter 5.)

Some essential oils can be applied directly to the skin, while others should only be used for their aromas. The most popular way to enjoy these oils is through a process called diffusion. Oil diffusers are devices that break down the essential oils so they are easily dispersed into the air, allowing the healing properties of their fragrances to enter your environment. There are four basic types of diffusers you can choose from: Nebulizing diffusers use pressurized air to disperse the oils into a mist. Evaporative diffusers are assisted by a small fan, which turns oil into a gas, allowing for evaporation into the air; electric diffusers have a similar process through utilizing heat. Ultrasonic or humidifying diffusers break up the oil molecules to create a fine mist. For a portable way to diffuse your essential oils, clay diffuser disks are a popular choice. These small, circular disks are usually made from terra-cotta and hold drops of your desired oil within their natural air pockets. Another popular method of enjoying essential oils is through shower steamers. Shower steamers are small, disk- or bar-shaped products that release essential oils into the steam of a shower, allowing aroma to diffuse into the space.

Always follow the instructions on the bottle, making sure not to exceed the recommended number of drops in each application. Due to their high concentration, it is not generally recommended or considered especially safe to swallow essential oils. To maximize their shelf life, keep oils in a cool, dark place, either at a cool room temperature or in the refrigerator. If you keep them in the fridge, place them in a sealed container to prevent the fragrance from affecting food. On average, essential oils will keep for six months to a year if kept cool. If oil becomes cloudy or begins to smell sour, throw it away.

Balsam

Description

Balsam is an aromatic tree resin that is used to make a variety of popular essential oils. These include balsam fir, whose aroma brings to mind a Christmas tree, and balsam of Peru, which smells like vanilla and cinnamon due to the presence of vanillin and cinnamic acid.

History and Lore

Balsam of Peru is a misnomer. Balsam comes from a tree of the genus *Myroxylon*, grown in Central and South America, primarily in El Salvador. Although balsam was collected all over Central and South America, it was shipped to Europe from Peru—hence the name. The first recorded export of balsam of Peru to Europe occurred in the seventeenth century. Long before that, the Maya were using balsam of Peru as incense for medicinal purposes.

Uses

Healing Uses

Incorporated into massage oil, balsam fir essential oil can soothe muscle aches and pains resulting from exercise, and its woodsy scent also aids the respiratory system. Balsam of Peru essential oil treats skin conditions, rheumatism, and respiratory issues, particularly those accompanied by a productive cough. It also has antiseptic and anti-inflammatory properties, making it helpful for healing wounds. However, some people are allergic to balsam of Peru, so proceed with caution when trying it for the first time.

Personal/Spiritual Growth

Balsam fir essential oil stimulates the mind while relaxing the body, creating a general sense of well-being. This is a wonderful essential oil for regulating mood swings, because it balances the forces within the body. It is especially helpful for balancing the sacral and heart chakras. When diffused during meditation, it serves as a grounding influence. Balsam of Peru essential oil reduces stress and mental exhaustion, but be aware that it may also bring up negative emotions that have been buried.

Basil

Description

Basil essential oil comes from the familiar culinary and medicinal herb discussed in Chapter 2. Varieties include sweet basil and holy basil, which are similar in appearance but have their own individual properties and uses. Sweet basil has a fresh, herbaceous aroma, while holy basil has a strong, spicy fragrance.

History and Lore

Holy basil, or tulsi, is native to India and is considered sacred in the Hindu religion. Hindus regard the plant as a manifestation of the goddess Tulsi and traditionally keep a holy basil plant in or near their homes. In Crete, basil was placed on windowsills to keep the devil away.

Uses

Healing Uses

Rub sweet basil essential oil on the abdomen to relieve indigestion, nausea, or stomach cramps. As an inhalation, both sweet basil and holy basil essential oils can be used to treat coughs, congestion, asthma, bronchitis, and sinus infections. Combined with massage, these oils relieve muscle aches and soreness.

Personal/Spiritual Growth

Inhaling the scent of basil refreshes and energizes the mind and eases headaches brought on by stress and tension. Sweet basil essential oil gives you the courage you need when undertaking new experiences. It also helps to clarify goals and plans. Holy basil essential oil opens your heart to receive the love of your partner, and it fortifies your sense of purpose, enabling you to focus on life's possibilities. Using this essential oil is also believed to ward off negative energy and act as spiritual protection.

Bergamot

Description

Bergamot essential oil comes from the rind of the citrus fruit of the bergamot tree (*Citrus bergamia*), which is commercially grown in southern Italy. The fruit is generally not eaten due to its sour flavor, but the oil has a fresh citrusy/floral scent. The word *bergamot* comes from Bergamo, a city in northern Italy where the tree was first cultivated.

History and Lore

Although it takes its name from an Italian city, the bergamot tree is actually native to Southeast Asia. Bergamot essential oil was first used in perfumes and cosmetics, and it was later valued for its medicinal properties. The oil is also an important ingredient in Earl Grey tea.

Uses

Healing Uses

Bergamot essential oil stimulates the mind and body, and aids in circulation and digestion. Applied topically, either as a spot treatment or incorporated in a carrier oil, it heals cuts, acne, cold sores, and psoriasis. Just be sure to avoid the sun for twenty-four hours after applying bergamot essential oil to the skin; exposure to ultraviolet rays can cause discoloration of the skin or sunburn.

Personal/Spiritual Growth

The scent of bergamot essential oil has a balancing, regenerating, and uplifting effect. Diffusing it builds confidence and enhances your mood, while helping you overcome obstacles and paving the way for new opportunities and growth. It is especially valuable for those dealing with depression, stress, tension, or fear. Use with massage or add to bathwater in these cases. This oil clears negativity from the aura, and is a great tool to use during meditation and daily spiritual cleansing rituals.

Carnation

Description

Carnation essential oil comes from the familiar flower (*Dianthus caryophyllus*), which is native to the Mediterranean region. The oil has a mildly sweet scent with notes of honey and spice, and it is typically found in "absolute" form, meaning that it was extracted using chemical solvents. The word *carnation* comes from the Latin *carnis*, meaning "flesh."

History and Lore

Flowers of the genus *Dianthus* are also known as "pinks." The word *pink* comes from the Middle English *pinken*, meaning "to push or prick"—a reference to the flower petals' jagged edges. The creation of carnation perfume is attributed to American perfumer Mary Chess, who, after becoming dissatisfied with commercial "toilet waters," began making her own fragrances using all-natural ingredients in the early 1930s.

Uses

Healing Uses

As a massage oil, carnation heals, softens, and rejuvenates the skin, and its soothing fragrance promotes relaxation. Used topically, it treats a variety of skin conditions, including eczema and rosacea, and soothes rashes and other irritations. Its scent brings energy and strength to those suffering from illness. This essential oil can also be diffused to ease symptoms of depression or to treat sleeplessness.

Personal/Spiritual Growth

This essential oil is spiritually uplifting and motivating. Inhaling carnation essential oil by placing a few drops in warm water fosters a feeling of openness and oneness with the universe, allowing the soul to relax and luxuriate in all experiences. Carnation essential oil facilitates contact with the deepest parts of ourselves so that we may sort through buried emotions and locate our true desires. Diffusing it creates a powerful aphrodisiac.

Cedar

Description

Cedar essential oil comes from the bark of the cedar tree, a coniferous evergreen that is native to the western Himalayas and the Mediterranean. Also called cedarwood, this oil has a woody, balsamic fragrance. Cedar wood is a natural moth repellent, which is why it is often used to make chests or closets for clothing storage.

History and Lore

The ancient Egyptians used cedar oil in the embalming process and as a perfume, and they used the wood to make sarcophagi. The ancient Greeks and Romans burned cedar as incense. Cedar is mentioned in both the Bible and the Talmud. Native Americans used cedar to enhance spiritual communication.

Uses

Healing Uses

Cedar essential oil is high in sesquiterpenes, natural compounds that stimulate the limbic system of the brain, which controls mood. For this reason, cedar oil is used in aromatherapy to reduce stress, assist with sleep, and support relaxation. Applied topically, this oil has antiseptic and anti-inflammatory properties, making it useful for treating skin issues and wounds. Rubbed on the joints, it soothes arthritis pain. It also acts as a natural insect repellent!

Personal/Spiritual Growth

This essential oil works with the heart chakra to invite self-acceptance and love. It banishes fear and instills a feeling of safety and security in yourself and in your environment. In addition to promoting relaxation, diffusing cedar essential oil may also improve focus and encouragement in the pursuit of long-held dreams and desires. Using this oil either as a room spray, in massage oil, or diffused elicits a grounding effect and allows for the dispersion of anxiety while connecting to higher realms.

Cinnamon

Description

Like the spice included in Chapter 2, cinnamon essential oil comes from certain tropical Asian trees of the genus *Cinnamomum*. There are two main varieties of this oil, one that comes from the leaves and one that comes from the bark, each with its own properties and uses. Both have a warm, spicy aroma, although the leaf oil is milder while the bark oil is more intense.

History and Lore

Despite cinnamon's widespread use throughout the ancient world, the Arab merchants who transported it managed to keep its origins secret until the early sixteenth century. European explorers, including Christopher Columbus and Gonzalo Pizarro, set out in search of the spice's source, and Portuguese traders finally discovered cinnamon in Ceylon (present-day Sri Lanka) around 1518.

Uses

Healing Uses

This essential oil supports cardiovascular and immune health and has a general calming effect. Cinnamon bark oil contains aldehydes, which soothe the nervous system. Eugenol, found in cinnamon leaf oil, has antiseptic and anesthetic properties when applied topically with a carrier oil. Diffused or utilized as a room spray around the home, it also battles mold and bacteria, improving air quality. Note that some people are allergic to cinnamon, and those with sensitive skin may find its "spicy" effect irritating.

Personal/Spiritual Growth

Cinnamon essential oil provides warmth, comfort, and mild stimulation. Use it with steam in the shower to open the solar plexus chakra and allow you to release old anger, resentment, frustration, and fear. Diffusing this oil is perfect for those who want to let go of the past and break old patterns. It also combats symptoms of depression and the habits of addiction. Cinnamon leaf oil as a room spray in particular boosts motivation and creativity.

Clary Sage

Description

Like the herb discussed in Chapter 2, clary sage is a plant in the genus *Salvia* that is native to the Mediterranean region. Clary sage essential oil comes from the leaves of this plant and is commonly used as a flavoring, in perfumery, and of course in aromatherapy. It has an earthy, herbaceous aroma.

History and Lore

The ancient Greek botanist and philosopher Theophrastus (371–287 B.C.E.) wrote extensively about the medicinal uses of clary sage. During the Middle Ages, clary sage was called "clear eye," due to the belief that it improved vision and protected the eyes from the effects of aging. In sixteenth-century England, this plant was sometimes substituted for hops in the production of beer.

Uses

Healing Uses

This is an excellent essential oil for women, as it assists with menstrual issues, childbirth, and symptoms of menopause, including mood swings. (Note that it should be avoided during the first months of pregnancy.) For cramps, massage the oil into the abdomen or lower back. Clary sage essential oil also benefits the skin and hair. Inhaling the scent has a calming effect and helps battle anxiety and depression. Adding this oil to a hair rinse fights dandruff.

Personal/Spiritual Growth

If you suffer from a racing mind, this oil can help keep you relaxed and focused. Adding this oil to clay tablets allows their scent to travel with you on the go. Inhaling this oil allows you to access inner wisdom without the distraction of too much thought. Place clary sage essential oil in the bath to open the root and sacral chakras, grounding the spirit in the body and boosting self-confidence and self-worth. Diffuse it to create a powerful aphrodisiac and enhance dreams.

Clove

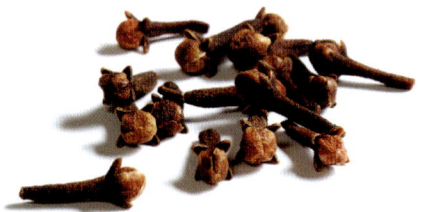

Description

Like the spice discussed in Chapter 2, clove essential oil comes from the flower bud of the evergreen tree *Syzygium aromaticum*. Clove leaf oil is also used, but its effect is milder than that of the flower bud. This essential oil has a sweet, spicy fragrance.

History and Lore

Cloves were found in Syrian pottery dating back to 1720 B.C.E. It was once believed that cinnamon was the bark, clove was the flower, and nutmeg was the fruit of the same tree. Cloves were one of the "big four" most valuable spices during the medieval era, along with nutmeg, cinnamon, and pepper.

Uses

Healing Uses

Clove boosts the immune and digestive systems and offers antioxidant support. Like cinnamon, clove contains large amounts of eugenol, a natural antiseptic and anesthetic. Eugenol is used today in the dental industry to numb the gums. To stimulate circulation and soothe muscular pain, rub clove essential oil on the affected area.

Personal/Spiritual Growth

Clove sets an aura of protection; to discourage unwanted spiritual influences, add it to clay tablets and carry them when entering an unfamiliar environment. You may even anoint charms or amulets with clove essential oil to boost their shielding properties. Either diffused or added to carrier oil, clove gets to the root of pain and discomfort— physical or emotional. It works with the solar plexus, heart, and throat chakras to fortify the self, expand inner strength, and draw out personal truth. Once the truth has emerged, you will feel inspired to take action in that direction.

Eucalyptus

Description

This essential oil comes from the leaves of the eucalyptus tree (*Eucalyptus globulus*), which is native to Australia and cultivated worldwide. The oil has a clean scent. The word *eucalyptus* comes from the Greek *kaluptos*, meaning "covered"—an allusion to the tree's capped flower bud.

History and Lore

Scientists estimate that the eucalyptus tree has survived on earth for 50 million years. Indigenous Australians have been using the branches of this ancient tree to make a ceremonial wind instrument called the didgeridoo for the past 1,500 years. The British botanist Sir Joseph Banks (1743–1820) is credited with introducing eucalyptus to the Western world.

Uses

Healing Uses

Eucalyptus leaves are rich in eucalyptol, a natural compound often used in mouthwashes and cough suppressants. Use eucalyptus essential oil with massage to soothe sore muscles, or rub it on the chest to clear up productive coughs and congestion. In some cases, it may ease the symptoms of asthma. Mixed with a carrier oil, it can moisturize hair. This oil is also an effective insect repellent, and can be used to treat insect bites and stings.

Personal/Spiritual Growth

This essential oil acts as a mental stimulant, battling exhaustion and sluggishness and boosting positive energy. Gently inhaling its fresh scent instantly rejuvenates the spirit, bringing relief to those struggling from melancholy or depression. Diffusing its oil immediately lowers stress levels and also encourages emotional balance. To clear a cluttered mind, add it to bathwater or steam in the shower. Eucalyptus essential oil opens the solar plexus and heart chakras.

Frankincense

Description

Frankincense is the aromatic resin of trees of the genus *Boswellia*, native to Africa and Asia. The word comes from the Old French *franc encens: franc,* meaning "free" or "pure," and *encens,* meaning "incense." *Incense* comes from the Latin verb *incendere,* "to set on fire." Frankincense essential oil has a woody, balsamic scent.

History and Lore

The ancient Egyptians used frankincense as incense, perfume, a cosmetic ingredient, an embalming preservative, and an offering to the gods. In the Bible, frankincense is one of the three gifts the wise men bring to the baby Jesus; the other two are gold and myrrh (see entry in this chapter).

Uses

Healing Uses

This essential oil benefits the skin and battles signs of premature aging. Applied topically with a carrier oil, it soothes sunburns, heals rashes, and prevents scarring, and it can also reduce the appearance of stretch marks. As an inhalation, it treats bronchitis. To ease joint and muscle pain, rub diluted frankincense essential oil on the affected area or add a few drops to your bath.

Personal/Spiritual Growth

Frankincense essential oil drives away negativity and brings peace and balance. This is a wonderful oil to diffuse during meditation, as it helps with grounding, clears your mind, and deepens your spiritual connections. It also enhances visions. Once you connect with your spiritual side, you can recognize and pursue your true purpose. Add this oil to bathwater when you feel overwhelmed. Adding a few drops to your household cleaner creates an uplifting environment.

Gardenia

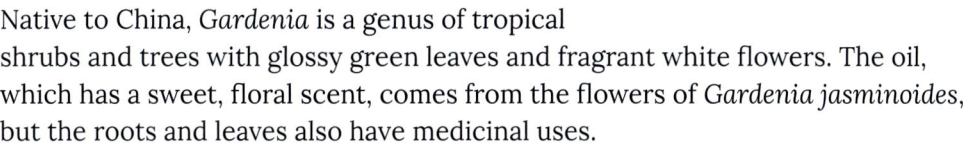

Description

Native to China, *Gardenia* is a genus of tropical shrubs and trees with glossy green leaves and fragrant white flowers. The oil, which has a sweet, floral scent, comes from the flowers of *Gardenia jasminoides*, but the roots and leaves also have medicinal uses.

History and Lore

This flower is named after Alexander Garden (1730–1791), a Scottish physician, botanist, and zoologist. It was previously, and is sometimes still, known as cape jasmine. Dried gardenia flowers have long been used in Chinese herbal medicine to treat anxiety, draw heat away from the body, and reduce swelling.

Uses

Healing Uses

This essential oil can be used as an anti-inflammatory, an antidepressant, or a sedative. It relieves tension and headaches, and may reduce symptoms of menopause. It can also ease dizziness. Added to bathwater, it has a relaxing effect and prevents insomnia. As an inhalation, gardenia essential oil eases respiratory issues, including sinus infections. Applied topically, it treats wounds and reduces swelling.

Personal/Spiritual Growth

Gardenia essential oil fosters love and harmony and works to improve mood. Diffusing it purifies your space, allowing for a sense of peaceful well-being. Add it to bathwater to ease a troubled mind. Use it with massage to bring peace and serenity. This oil stimulates the heart chakra and can also be used as an aphrodisiac, particularly in women. It is thought to strengthen the romantic connection in partnerships. Diffused in meditation, it heightens spiritual awareness and the ability to connect to inner wisdom.

Geranium

Description

This essential oil comes from the leaves of the geranium plant, a member of the genus *Pelargonium*, which comprises hundreds of species. One of the most prominent sources of this essential oil is *Pelargonium graveolens*, native to southern Africa and introduced by French colonists to the island of Réunion in the Indian Ocean. Although the oil comes from the leaves and not the flowers, the fragrance is often compared to that of a rose.

History and Lore

There are actually two genera of geraniums: *Pelargonium* and *Geranium*. When the Swedish botanist Carl Linnaeus (1707–1778) created his plant taxonomy, he grouped all of these plants together. The genera have since been separated, but both are still generally known as geraniums. These plants are sometimes called storksbill or cranesbill, due to the beak-like shape of the seed capsule.

Uses

Healing Uses

This essential oil supports the circulatory and nervous systems, and it is also excellent for the skin. It heals wounds and treats a number of skin conditions, including acne, eczema, and athlete's foot. Use it as a topical insect repellent or to relieve the itch and discomfort of insect bites. As a massage oil, it soothes sore muscles. Sprinkle geranium essential oil in a foot bath for a healing foot soak.

Personal/Spiritual Growth

Geranium essential oil has a strong feminine energy. Diffusing this oil soothes and nurtures the inner child, fostering a sense of calm and peace. It lifts the spirit and helps to release negative memories and stress. This essential oil provides comfort and reassurance in times of distress or disappointment. Added to bathwater, this oil eases irritability. An inhalation before bed will relax the mind and prevent insomnia.

Jasmine

Description

Jasmine essential oil comes from the white or yellow flowers of vines or shrubs of the genus *Jasminum*, mainly *Jasminum officinale*, which are native to Asia. In this case, *essential oil* is a misnomer, as the flowers are too delicate to withstand the distillation process. Instead, this oil is an absolute, which means it is extracted using chemical solvents. It is expensive due to the large number of flowers needed to produce it. This oil has a strong, sweet, floral aroma.

History and Lore

Jasmine absolute is called the king of oils (rose is the queen). A related plant, *Jasminum sambac*, is very important in India. It is incorporated into cultural traditions and ceremonies, and women often wear the blossoms in their hair. Jasmine is the national flower of Pakistan, where it is known as chameli. Jasmine tea is extremely popular in China.

Uses

Healing Uses

This oil eases cramps and mood swings associated with PMS and menstruation. It is too strong to be used during pregnancy, but it is excellent for childbirth (use it to massage the lower abdomen during labor). Jasmine essential oil has long been used for breastfeeding mothers to encourage lactation and reduce skin irritation. Jasmine oil benefits the skin and acts as an antidepressant. It is also a well-known aphrodisiac.

Personal/Spiritual Growth

Jasmine oil is associated with female energy, particularly sexual energy. Diffuse it to promote the expression of intimate feelings. When sprayed around a room, it boosts confidence and has a general uplifting quality. In times of confusion, jasmine essential oil brings the true wishes of the heart to light. Add it to bathwater to relieve stress. Jasmine essential oil is said to attract the attention of higher vibrational spiritual beings in meditation and prayer.

Lavender

Description

A flowering plant in the mint family, lavender (*Lavandula angustifolia*) is the quintessential aromatherapy plant. Its refreshing floral scent makes for a relaxing essential oil, and it also has many medicinal and household uses. Lavender is native to the Mediterranean region.

History and Lore

The ancient Greeks used lavender in embalming practices. The ancient Greeks and Romans used lavender for healing as well as for cleansing purposes. In 1910, while working in the lab at his family's cosmetics company, the French chemist and scholar René-Maurice Gattefossé (1881–1950) burned his hand and then plunged it into the nearest tub of liquid, lavender essential oil. Later, he was astonished to see how quickly his burn healed, and with very little scarring.

Uses

Healing Uses

The scent of lavender is extremely relaxing. It relieves headaches, tension, anxiety, and insomnia, making it a wonderful addition to bathwater or a pillow. Lavender essential oil has anti-inflammatory and antiseptic properties, and applied topically, this oil helps heal wounds, burns, eczema, acne, and other skin irritations. With massage, it soothes muscle aches and reduces swelling.

Personal/Spiritual Growth

This is the ultimate essential oil for peace and calm, allowing for relaxation and restful sleep. It also lifts the spirit and brings emotional balance with its nurturing, reassuring quality. This makes it especially helpful to those dealing with depression. Lavender also unblocks the third eye chakra, quieting the mind and facilitating higher states of awareness. Diffusing lavender oil in meditation activates the crown chakra, allowing for higher consciousness connection.

Lemon

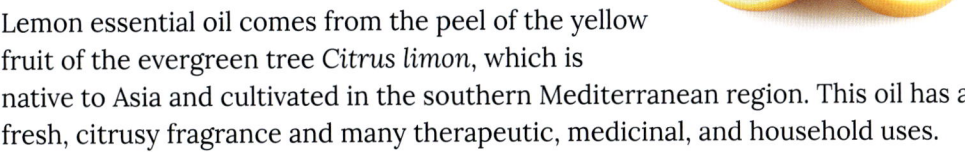

Description

Lemon essential oil comes from the peel of the yellow fruit of the evergreen tree *Citrus limon*, which is native to Asia and cultivated in the southern Mediterranean region. This oil has a fresh, citrusy fragrance and many therapeutic, medicinal, and household uses.

History and Lore

The exact origin of the lemon tree is undetermined, but many think it may have been northwestern India. Arab traders then brought the plant to the Middle East and Africa, and from there it traveled to Europe. Until about the tenth century, the lemon tree was mainly an ornamental plant. After that, it developed culinary and medicinal uses, such as a treatment for scurvy, a disease resulting from a deficiency of vitamin C.

Uses

Healing Uses

Lemon essential oil has antiseptic and astringent qualities, making it excellent for the skin as well as household cleaning. Mixed with tea tree oil or on its own, lemon oil makes a great alternative to chemical cleaning agents. Diffusing it boosts energy, fights fatigue, and improves mood. It also calms the stomach, relieves nausea, and improves digestion. Avoid sun exposure after topical use of this oil, as it can "bleach" hair and cause skin irritation such as blisters and burns.

Personal/Spiritual Growth

Enjoying this uplifting essential oil's scent clears away negative emotions and fosters a cheerful mood. It serves to purify the mind, body, and soul. As a room spray, it also enhances focus and concentration and helps with problem-solving and decision-making. Diffusing lemon oil balances the solar plexus chakra and is a great tool during personal transformations.

Mint

Description

Mint essential oil comes from the leaves of plants of the genus *Mentha*, including peppermint (*Mentha piperita*), spearmint (*Mentha spicata*), and bergamot mint (*Mentha citrata*). Most will recognize the fresh, sharp aroma of this essential oil as that of chewing gum, toothpaste, liniments for sore muscles, and other common products.

History and Lore

The word *mint* comes from the Greek *minthe*, which is also the name of a nymph in Greek mythology. According to the story, Minthe angered Persephone, who turned the nymph into a pungent plant as punishment. Native to Europe, Asia, and Australia, mint plants are cultivated in temperate regions worldwide.

Uses

Healing Uses

Mint essential oil contains menthol, a natural compound that acts as a topical anesthetic. Rub on sore muscles to cool and soothe the area, or on the abdomen to relieve intestinal discomfort. Gently inhaled, this oil also eases nausea, calms stomach cramps, and supports digestion. Mint oil is regarded as one of the best essential oils for colds, coughs, and other respiratory conditions. Placing it in an oil diffuser or adding it to steam in the shower also alleviates stress and conditions resulting from stress, such as headaches and insomnia.

Personal/Spiritual Growth

This essential oil refreshes and revives the spirit, eliminating fatigue and boosting energy. It is helpful to inhale mint oil when you need a boost of motivation. When seeking to cleanse a space of stagnant energy, diffusing peppermint oil supports awareness and replaces negativity with positivity. Spearmint oil cools heated emotions and brings inner peace and calm. Bergamot mint oil inspires spontaneity. Add any of these to bathwater for emotional balance.

Myrrh

Description

Myrrh is the aromatic gum resin of trees and shrubs of the genus *Commiphora*, native to northeastern Africa and the Middle East. Historically, it has been used to make perfume, incense, and medicine. Myrrh essential oil has a rich, woody aroma.

History and Lore

The ancient Egyptians used myrrh in embalming practices. The first known medical use of myrrh (as topical application for wounds) is documented in a Greek text dating back to the fifth century B.C.E. In the Bible, myrrh is one of the three gifts the wise men bring to the baby Jesus; the other two are frankincense (see entry in this chapter) and gold.

Uses

Healing Uses

Myrrh essential oil supports the circulatory, nervous, and digestive systems. It also eases chest congestion and coughs; for this purpose, use it as an inhalation or rub it on the chest. This oil has astringent, antiseptic, and anti-inflammatory properties, making it helpful for treating wounds. Due to its antimicrobial properties, it can inhibit bacteria growth and may assist with treating oral infections. Used in a hot compress, it draws out infection.

Personal/Spiritual Growth

The high levels of sesquiterpenes in myrrh essential oil stimulate the brain's limbic system, which controls mood. Inhaling the fragrance of this oil has a calming and uplifting effect, fostering a sense of peace and tranquility. It encourages letting go of old wounds and allows for the forgiveness that is necessary for moving forward. It's useful in meditation as a grounding oil. Try rubbing it on all chakras to establish spiritual balance.

Orange Blossom

Description

Orange blossom essential oil, also called neroli, comes from the flower of the bitter orange tree *Citrus aurantium*. Like lemon essential oil, it has therapeutic, medicinal, and household uses. The oil has a sweet, citrusy fragrance.

History and Lore

The ancient Egyptians used orange blossom oil for healing and ceremonial purposes. French-born Marie Anne de la Trémoille (1642–1722), a princess of Nerola, Italy, is credited with introducing bitter orange oil as a fashionable fragrance; hence the name *neroli*. It has been speculated that this oil is one of the ingredients in the secret recipe for the soft drink Coca-Cola.

Uses

Healing Uses

Orange blossom essential oil supports the digestive and nervous systems and benefits the skin. Rub it on the abdomen to ease indigestion, and massage it into dry areas to moisturize and rejuvenate skin. Orange blossom oil may help lower blood pressure and reduce the body's production of cortisol. As an inhalation, it is an effective treatment for insomnia or disrupted sleep, and it can help lift symptoms of depression and relieve anxiety.

Personal/Spiritual Growth

This rich essential oil fosters happiness and revitalizes the spirit. It opens the sacral chakra, the source of confidence and self-worth. It releases insecurities and fosters a sense of inner peace and harmony. Diffusing orange blossom essential oil in your space uplifts the vibration of the home or office and clears energetic clutter. Keeping your mind and body firmly rooted in the present, it allows you to harness your own personal power to manifest your desires. Enjoy it added to bathwater for a quick mood boost.

Patchouli

Description

This essential oil comes from the leaves of the shrub *Pogostemon cablin*, a member of the mint family. Native to Southeast Asia, this plant is extensively cultivated in India, Malaysia, China, Indonesia, the Philippines, and South America. The oil has a musky, earthy aroma.

History and Lore

In the eighteenth and nineteenth centuries, Indian silk traders packed their cloth in patchouli to keep moths away, leading many to believe that the cloth itself had a rich scent. Both patchouli oil and incense became enormously popular in the United States and Europe during the hippie movement of the 1960s and 1970s.

Uses

Healing Uses

Patchouli essential oil is an excellent remedy for skin issues. It hydrates and nourishes dry, chapped skin and clears up conditions such as acne and eczema. Its antiseptic properties can prevent infection, and it is beneficial for small cuts and scrapes. Applied to the hair and scalp, it alleviates oiliness and dandruff. As an inhalation, this oil soothes the nerves, relieves stress, and fights insomnia. It is also a powerful aphrodisiac.

Personal/Spiritual Growth

Patchouli essential oil balances the mind, body, and spirit. It also helps reveal the path around obstacles so that goals become more attainable. Diffusing patchouli oil clears the aura and absorbs negative energy. Use it topically during meditation to quiet the mind and ground and center spiritual awareness in the body. Patchouli is also thought to be a powerful aid during astral travel and other out-of-body spiritual experiences. Add it to bathwater to ease mental exhaustion and emotional stress. With massage, this oil boosts sexual energy.

Pine

Description

Pine essential oil comes from the needles of the coniferous tree *Pinus sylvestris*, also called Scots pine. These trees are widely cultivated for ornamental use as well as for their timber and resinous sap, used to make turpentine and pine tar. With its invigorating, woodsy scent, this oil has therapeutic, medicinal, and household cleaning uses.

History and Lore

Native to Europe and Asia, the pine tree became a popular Christmas tree choice in the United States in the 1950s, despite the fact that it does not grow well in many areas of the country due to climate and soil differences. Native Americans chewed pine needles to treat scurvy; chewing releases the oil, which is rich in vitamin C. Stuffing a mattress with pine needles helps keep lice and fleas at bay.

Uses

Healing Uses

Pine essential oil has many of the same properties as eucalyptus (see entry in this chapter). Used in massage or bathwater, it soothes sore muscles and joints. As an inhalation, it treats respiratory problems, acting as an expectorant to clear congestion. Its anti-inflammatory properties make pine oil helpful for the relief of joints aching from arthritis. It is also an effective stimulant, boosting metabolism and increasing energy levels.

Personal/Spiritual Growth

Pine essential oil clears and refreshes the mind and grounds the body. It balances the heart and sacral chakras, fostering inner peace and self-love. When diffused, the powerful scent moves the spirit while allowing for acceptance and the acknowledgment of inner wisdom. Meditate with this oil to lift a dark mood and enhance spiritual focus.

Rosemary

Description

Rosemary essential oil comes from the leaves of the herb discussed in Chapter 2. The word *rosemary* has roots in the Latin *ros marinus*: *ros*, meaning "dew"—perhaps from the oil glands on the undersides of the leaves—and *marinus*, meaning "of the sea." This oil has a strong, herbaceous fragrance.

History and Lore

Rosemary essential oil is a staple in traditional Indian medicine. Before refrigeration, this herb was often used as a food preservative. It is said that inhaling the scent of rosemary essential oil brings back long-forgotten memories. The Swiss German physician and botanist Paracelsus (1493–1541) valued rosemary oil for its powerful healing abilities.

Uses

Healing Uses

Applied topically, rosemary essential oil stimulates hair growth, conditions the scalp and hair, and treats dandruff and split ends. It also benefits the skin, particularly in cases of acne and eczema. Used with steam in the shower, this oil supports digestion and relieves stomach cramps, constipation, and bloating. Massage the oil into sore muscles to relax them. Rosemary oil repels bugs and can even be used as a natural pesticide when sprayed on other garden plants or as a repellent on your own skin.

Personal/Spiritual Growth

Rosemary essential oil overcomes fatigue and rejuvenates the mind. Diffusing it in your home or office provides focus and improved mental function, all the while dispelling negativity from the space. It also brings clarity, renews enthusiasm, and inspires creativity. This oil will restore your passion for life and help you follow your true path. It also serves to remind us that we are spiritual beings and that there is more to life than what is seen.

Sandalwood

Description

Sandalwood essential oil comes from the fragrant inner heartwood of trees of the genus *Santalum*, particularly Indian sandalwood (*Santalum album*) and Australian sandalwood (*Santalum spicatum*). This oil has a warm, woody aroma—the Australian variety is milder than the Indian.

History and Lore

It takes forty years for an Indian sandalwood tree to reach maturity and produce essential oil of the highest potency. Due to illegal logging, there is currently a shortage of Indian sandalwood trees, which has caused Australian sandalwood to become more prevalent on the market. Both varieties have a long history of use as incense, perfume, and medicine.

Uses

Healing Uses

Sandalwood essential oil is high in sesquiterpenes, natural compounds that stimulate the limbic system of the brain. This area of the brain controls breathing, heart rate, blood pressure, memory, stress levels, and hormone balance. Gently inhaling this oil has a relaxing effect, making it an excellent sleep remedy. Applied topically, it has antiseptic, anti-inflammatory, and astringent qualities. As a shower steamer, sandalwood essential oil is valuable to use when fighting a viral infection or needing to reduce a pesky cough.

Personal/Spiritual Growth

This essential oil warms the heart and fortifies the inner self. It assists in overcoming vulnerability and emotional challenges. Working with the root and sacral chakras, massaging with this oil facilitates grounding and increases confidence and sensuality. It's an excellent support to take on the go as a clay diffuser to deal with self-doubt. This is an excellent essential oil to diffuse during meditation, as it encourages quiet focus and brings the attention inward.

Tea Tree

Description

Tea tree essential oil comes from the leaves of the melaleuca tree (*Melaleuca alternifolia*), which is native to Australia. Also called melaleuca oil, this essential oil has a fresh, medicinal aroma.

History and Lore

The discovery of the melaleuca tree is commonly attributed to the British explorer Captain James Cook (1728–1779) and his sailors, who brewed an infusion using the tree's leaves to fight scurvy; hence the name *tea tree*. However, Indigenous Australians were using the leaves to treat headaches and respiratory problems long before Cook arrived.

Uses

Healing Uses

Tea tree essential oil is excellent for the skin and can be applied topically to treat acne, wounds, burns, infections, and insect bites. It also has antiviral properties, making it an effective treatment for colds and flu. It can even act as an alternative to chemical-based hand sanitizer. Its antibacterial properties make it an impressive underarm deodorant. As an inhalation, tea tree essential oil acts as a stimulant, increasing circulation and boosting the immune system. Used during massage, this oil soothes muscle aches.

Personal/Spiritual Growth

This essential oil boosts energy and renews optimism and self-confidence. It stimulates the mind as well as the body, sharpening focus and refreshing thought processes. Diffused in a space, it repels negativity and promotes balance. Tea tree essential oil helps to heal emotional wounds, releasing feelings of distrust, guilt, and shame. Add it to an amulet to summon strength. It is particularly valuable in clearing blockages in chakras, especially the third eye.

Vanilla

Description

Vanilla essential oil is derived from the dried brown pods of *Vanilla planifolia*, a climbing vine with trumpet-shaped white flowers related to the orchid. Because this oil is extracted using a solvent, it is technically an absolute, not an essential oil. It has a sweet, balsamic scent.

History and Lore

The Totonac people of the eastern coastal and mountainous regions of Mexico were the first to cultivate vanilla and were the world's main vanilla producers until the mid-nineteenth century. The Spanish explorers who arrived in Mexico in the early sixteenth century gave the plant its name: The Spanish *vainilla* is a diminutive of *vaina*, meaning "sheath"—a reference to the shape of the seedpod.

Uses

Healing Uses

Vanilla absolute is calming and comforting. It has a relaxing effect on the mind and body and is commonly used to relieve stress, tension, anxiety, and panic attacks. It can also relieve symptoms of depression. Used in massage, vanilla absolute is a powerful aphrodisiac. It's also an effective deodorant, and eradicates lingering odors around the house. The antimicrobial properties of vanilla absolute make it a great option for use in skin and hair care.

Personal/Spiritual Growth

This warming absolute dissolves anger and frustration, relaxes the mind, and fosters a sense of inner peace. It stimulates the sacral chakra, boosting self-confidence and encouraging intimacy. It also has a very sensual quality; use with a partner to deepen physical connection by adding its oil to candles or using as a room spray. Carry it on a clay diffuser to attract love in all its forms, including self-love, friendships, and romantic connections. Diffused in meditation, it brings the spirit into balance.

Ylang-Ylang

Description

Ylang-ylang essential oil comes from the fragrant flowers of the tropical Asian tree *Cananga odorata*. It is native to the Philippines and Indonesia, but it is also grown in Polynesia, Melanesia, Micronesia, and the Comoro Islands. The oil has a sweet, floral scent.

History and Lore

In Indonesia, ylang-ylang flower petals are strewn on the beds of newlywed couples. In the Philippines, ylang-ylang flowers are used to adorn religious figures, and women wear strings of the flowers around their necks. Ylang-ylang oil is a main ingredient in the famous perfume Chanel No. 5.

Uses

Healing Uses

Ylang-ylang essential oil is very calming and relaxing, making it effective for treating stress-related high blood pressure. It also relieves sleeplessness and symptoms of depression. Applied topically, this oil benefits the skin and supports hair growth. Its scent acts as a deodorant and it aids those suffering from dry skin. Added to bathwater, it soothes symptoms of PMS and menopause, including irritability and mood swings. When applied to the wrists and neck, it is an excellent energizer to fight fatigue or body aches.

Personal/Spiritual Growth

This essential oil is perfect for those who have trouble forgiving or being kind to themselves. It aids in releasing negative emotions such as anger and fear and boosts positive emotions, self-esteem, and spiritual awareness. As a room spray, ylang-ylang oil is a spiritual protector, blocking unwanted thoughts and energies from entering the mindspace. Diffusing ylang-ylang works with the heart chakra to increase self-love. It also encourages harmony by balancing male and female energies in the body.

5

The Power of Fire and Light

The element of fire is a powerful component of energy healing. Fire and light represent transformation and are symbolic of the stripping away of the material world to reveal a spiritual truth. Fire gives way for new beginnings, and the explosion of creativity born of passion in a person's life as they forge new paths ahead. It also provides a sense of courage and willpower, and is fundamental in many of the energy healing rituals and practices humans have conducted for thousands of years.

Fire as a symbol represents release, purification, and a cleansing of negativity. The feeling of freedom released when you watch a list burn at a full moon ceremony can fill you with a sense of surrender to the coming transformation in life. Light as a symbol represents truth, energy, and protection from the shadows we live among. A candle burning during a meditation provides a sense of accompaniment while navigating your own shadows. In energy healing, fire burns through patterns that no longer serve you so you can make room for what belongs. The fascination with fire's power lives deeply within us as we crave the revelations it shines its light upon. In this chapter, you'll discover various ways of harnessing fire and light to benefit your mind, body, and spirit.

Aromatherapy

Description

Aromatherapy, the holistic practice of using plant essential oils to promote well-being via scent, is an ancient practice with many modern ways to experience its benefits. Through inhalation, internal use, and topical application (depending on what types of oils or aromas are being used), aromatherapy can support emotional, mental, and even physical health.

History and Lore

The practice of aromatherapy as we know it today has roots in numerous ancient civilizations. In Ayurveda, which is ancient Indian medicine, aromatherapy was used to balance the doshas, or body's energies. In ancient Greece, Hippocrates, known as the father of Western medicine, promoted the power of aroma, specifically lavender and rosemary, to heal the body and mind. Native Americans burned specific plants such as sage and cedar in spiritual rituals in order to cleanse energy fields. The aromatic molecules released when heating the essential oils extracted from plants have positive effects on mood and overall well-being. A French chemist named René-Maurice Gattefossé (1881–1950) is known as the father of aromatherapy, and much of what we see today has been shaped by his work. The research and experiments he conducted laid the groundwork for modern practices. The Austrian-born biochemist Marguerite Maury (1895–1968) subsequently developed massage techniques incorporating essential oils that are still in use.

Uses

The most popular ways to introduce aromatherapy are by applying it to the skin or inhaling it from a diffuser. The oils used are often referred to as essential oils and come from a plant's flowers, seeds, leaves, and woods. Aromatherapy may help boost mood, reduce inflammation, and even kill bacteria and viruses. The various tools available to experience the healing scents include diffusers, misters, inhalers, bathing salts, body oils, lotions, or masks for the skin.

Different oils provide a variety of physical, emotional, and spiritual benefits. Lavender oil can be utilized to promote sleep and alleviate stress. You can reap its benefits by adding water to lavender oil to make a room spray, or by putting it in a bath for soaking. A cotton swab dipped in tea tree oil can help with acne, while smelling eucalyptus oil can loosen congestion. Diffused lemon oil is helpful with easing nausea, and lemongrass oil is known to help lower blood sugar. Connection to the chakras is often another benefit to working with aromatherapy. Rose oil can help open the heart chakra, whereas your third eye is aligned with frankincense. Incorporating essential oils into your meditations can provide clarity and peace when reaching higher realms of consciousness.

Before you begin, carefully research which aromatherapy oils work best with which ailments and in which ways, as the incorrect usage of them can cause certain side effects. Tea tree oil, for example, can be toxic to pets and children when used incorrectly, and lemon oil can increase your risk of sunburn.

Candles

Description

There's a basic structure to a candle: a solid mass of tallow, wax, or another fatty substance with a wick running through the center that is burned to provide light. But these simple objects come in all shapes and sizes, from pillars to tapers to votives, and there are seemingly countless applications for candles in cultural, religious, and other traditions. They are also used in various healing methods, including candle therapy, aromatherapy, and color therapy (see entries in this chapter). The word *candle* comes from the Latin *candere*, meaning "to shine."

History and Lore

The ancient Egyptians are believed to have been the first to make and use candles, although their candles did not have wicks and were instead more like torches, made of reeds dipped in melted tallow (animal fat). The Romans are credited with being the first to use wicked candles, which they made by dipping rolled papyrus in melted tallow or beeswax. Wicked candles were also used in ancient China, Japan, and India. Hanukkah, the Jewish holiday that centers on the lighting of candles, dates back to the second century B.C.E.

Uses

In addition to providing light, candles have been used throughout history in spiritual ceremonies and traditions as well as for healing and therapeutic purposes. Candle therapy is a practice that unites the body, mind, and spirit. Focusing or meditating on a flame has a relaxing effect that has been shown to reduce stress and can even improve conditions such as high blood pressure. Scented candles may be especially effective in these practices. You can also buy unscented candles and add your own scents to them using flower essences or essential oils (see Chapters 3 and 4). In the metaphysical realm, candles are often used for the purposes of cleansing, manifestation, and protection. Anointing your candles with different oils and using them alongside crystals creates a customized spiritual use. Additionally, you can amplify a candle's power by reciting a mantra while lighting it or inscribing the wax with intentions or prayers.

Color Therapy

Description

Color therapy, also called chromotherapy, is an alternative healing method that uses colored light to balance the energies of the body. Although color therapy is not a widely used practice, it is gaining popularity in the holistic and natural therapy realms with patients suffering from depression, those recovering from stroke, and others. Tools used in color therapy may include lamps, candles, gemstones, crystal or glass prisms, and colored eye lenses.

History and Lore

The use of color therapy goes all the way back to the ancient Egyptians and Greeks, who used colored stones and crystals for healing purposes. The Persian philosopher and scientist Avicenna (980–1037) wrote extensively about the importance of color in medical diagnosis and treatment. He believed that red increased circulation, blue slowed the blood, and yellow reduced pain and inflammation. In the Hindu, yogic, and other traditions, each of the chakras, or energy centers in the body, corresponds with a different color: The root chakra is red, the sacral or base chakra is orange, the solar plexus or navel chakra is yellow, the heart chakra is green, the throat chakra is blue, the third eye chakra is indigo, and the crown chakra is violet.

Uses

Color therapy has been shown to be an effective treatment for a wide range of illnesses and conditions. Blue light is used to treat neonatal jaundice. Exposure to white light benefits those who suffer from seasonal affective disorder (SAD). In athletes, red light is shown to provide quick bursts of energy, while blue light assists with steadier energy needs. Pink light has a tranquilizing effect and can be used to calm aggression, hostility, or anxiety. Yellow stimulates the mind and body and can benefit those dealing with depression.

Color therapy can have spiritual advantages as well. Visualizing the color indigo, for example, can support relaxation and increase intuition. In meditation, mindfully breathing while envisioning a specific color entering the body upon each inhale integrates the energy of the color into the body, promoting balance and wellness. You may even want to surround yourself in a specific color decor, home lighting, or clothing that reflects the energy you wish to assimilate.

Incense

Description

Incense is a natural substance, often combined with essential oils, that releases an aromatic smoke when burned. There are two main types: combustible (or direct-burning), which burns on its own, and noncombustible (or indirect-burning), which requires a separate heat source. The most common form of combustible incense is paste formed around a bamboo stick, but it may also be paste formed into a cone shape. Either form is lit and then the flame is blown out, allowing the resulting ember to smolder. Noncombustible incense is usually in whole, powdered, or paste form and heated on charcoal or in a container over a flame or coals. Often incense will be made up of two or more ingredients; for example, the Indian incense *nag champa* contains sandalwood and floral extracts. The word *incense* comes from the Latin verb *incendere*, which means "to set on fire."

History and Lore

The ancient Egyptians burned resins as incense for their pleasant scent and also incorporated them into their ceremonial and embalming processes. The ancient Greeks and Romans also burned resins as incense and used them during cremations. Frankincense and myrrh (see entries in Chapter 4) were among the first resins burned as incense, and aromatic herbs and spices also have been used throughout history for this purpose. The Chinese have been burning items such as cinnamon and sandalwood as incense since as far back as 2000 B.C.E.

Uses

There are many reasons to burn incense, but perhaps the simplest is that it smells good. You may burn incense to counteract a foul odor or to refresh the air in an unventilated area or sickroom. Many believe that the smoke of incense can also clear away negative energies, making way for new, positive energy. For this reason, it is recommended that you burn incense in a new home to remove any negative influences from the previous owners. Rosemary, sage, and thyme are favorites for cleansing and purifying a space. Incense burning is also a great accompaniment to meditation—frankincense and sandalwood are excellent for this. Mindfully choosing your incense is helpful when incorporating it into energy healing practices.

Light Therapy

Description

Light therapy, also known as phototherapy, is a treatment that consists of exposure to daylight or artificial light. It is often prescribed in cases of seasonal affective disorder (SAD), nonseasonal depression, delayed sleep-phase disorder, and certain skin conditions, including psoriasis, eczema, neonatal jaundice, and even skin cancer.

History and Lore

Light therapy, once called heliotherapy, is not a new idea. The ancient Egyptians discovered that exposure to the sun could disinfect and prevent disease. The ancient Greeks built structures called solaria for sunbathing, with the purpose of treating skin ailments and increasing health and vitality. The Incas of Peru worshipped the sun god, Inti, and had many ceremonies and rituals based around the sun. In India, the solar deity Surya is important in the Hindu religion, and worship includes a series of "sun salutations" performed at dawn.

Uses

Those who suffer from the "winter blues" may actually have seasonal affective disorder (SAD), a mood disorder caused by lack of exposure to sunlight and characterized by low energy and symptoms of depression, such as sleeping too much. Even if getting outdoors is not an option, you can use an artificial light box indoors to "cheer up" your brain. This treatment may also help those with delayed sleep phase syndrome, who typically don't fall asleep until the early hours of the morning, and then they are too tired to wake up for school or work. Light therapy upon awakening has been shown to help regulate sleep phases; this is often done in combination with light restriction in the evening. While artificial light boxes designed for these conditions filter out ultraviolet (UV) light, light therapy treatments for certain skin conditions require UV light to be effective. In these cases, the light exposure slows down cell growth and inhibits inflammation related to conditions like psoriasis and eczema.

Smoke Cleansing

Description

The ancient practice of producing smoke by burning specific plants to create protection, cleansing, and other positive effects has been seen in countless cultures and religions. Smudging, while similar, is considered distinct due to its cultural roots and ceremonial traditions, and was specifically developed by Native Americans as a ritual connecting smoke and spirituality. Cleansing with smoke has been adopted by a wider movement of energy healers and holistic practitioners.

History and Lore

Archaeological evidence suggests that the use of smoke for ceremonies can be traced back to prehistoric times. Romans and Greeks burned bay leaves and rosemary for purification and to keep away evil spirits. In China and India, smoke has had an important role in rituals of meditation and spiritual connection. In medieval Europe, it was common practice to burn juniper and other herbs with the hope of warding off disease. The smoke cleansing seen in much of the New Age movements is based on the Native American practice called the Sacred Smoke Bowl Blessing. White sage (see Chapter 2 for information on proper harvesting and ethical practices) is the most popular herb used; however, it is also seen with cedar, sweet grass, and lavender. And the Plains tribes of North America used tobacco in smoke cleansing rituals.

Uses

Cleansing with smoke brings in positive, high-vibrational energy while eliminating anything stagnant or negative. It is helpful in cleansing the aura as it lifts away impurities, stress, and sadness. Smoke cleansing is also thought to assist in the physical body's healing process and provide cleansing protection for a home or office. Different herbs harbor specialized results: Sage is often burned for strength and clarity, cedar for eliminating unwanted spiritual intrusions, and tobacco for inviting gratitude. The sticks used in smoke cleansing may be one kind of herb or several, and either tied together or placed in a ceremonial bowl when burned. If practicing smoke cleansing in an enclosed space, make sure to keep doors and windows open to allow for the smoke to usher out unwanted energies. Be sure to return the ashes to the earth when done as a sign of respect.

6

The Power of Sound

In our modern world, we are inundated with constant noise. The whooshing of traffic, the buzzing and dinging of our devices, and the hum of heating and cooling systems have become the norm. We have grown so accustomed to this constant clamor we don't even notice it anymore, and our minds find ways to work around the distraction as best as they possibly can. The disarray causes energetic discord, and a subsequent inability to connect with the quiet voice within. The distraction of noise is one you can learn to tune out, and by using energy healing tools, begin to tune back into your body.

For our human selves, the ubiquitous din is not a natural state of being. Our bodies evolved and developed at a time before highways and electricity. The sounds of nature were our only noises—wind in the trees, rushing streams, insect buzzes, animal calls—and those sounds, along with pure silence, are what our brains and bodies find comforting and natural. It is no wonder our bodies endure a constant state of fight or flight, our nervous systems unequipped to deal with the commotion we now live within.

Exposing your body to healing sounds allows your energy to align and balance. Mindful moments listening to Hz frequencies, participating in a local sound bath, or even ringing a cheerful bell when feeling stressed may have you finding an inner calm you've never been able to access before. Using sound can positively impact your daily life in new ways, such as better sleep cycles, reduced anxiety, and a sense of community when this hobby is shared with others.

In this chapter, we will discuss the power of sound to transport you to a quieter, simpler time—or perhaps deeper inside your own mind. The instruments and practices discussed in these pages have long histories and multiple applications in various spiritual traditions. Perhaps you'd like to add chanting to your yoga practice or incorporate flute music into your meditation routine. Maybe you'll even try your hand at learning a new instrument or join a group activity such as a drum circle. However you choose to experiment with these powerful sounds, they have the power to restore balance and peace to your personal energy.

Bell

Description

A bell is a hollow musical instrument that produces a ringing tone when struck. It is usually made of metal, but it may also be ceramic, glass, or another material. A bell is typically cup-shaped with a flared opening, and the striking implement may be a "tongue" inside the bell or a separate mallet or hammer used on the outside of the bell. Tubular bells, or chimes, are a common variation. Bells are often associated with religion and spirituality, but they may also be used in healing and other practices.

History and Lore

The earliest evidence of bells dates back to the third millennium B.C.E. in Neolithic China. These pottery bells were replaced with metal bells about a thousand years later. Bells have long played a prominent role in both Eastern and Western religions, including Buddhism, Hinduism, and Christianity. Historically, they have been used as church bells that call worshippers to services, as instruments used in musical performances, and as tools in agricultural and domestic labor, either to help keep track of animals or to call workers in from the fields. The largest existing bell, the Tsar Bell, weighs more than 200 tons and is on display in Moscow's Kremlin Museum.

Uses

Bells have many musical and practical uses, but they can also be incorporated into spiritual practices. For example, in meditation, the sound of a bell may help keep your mind energy focused in the present. Bells may be also used to mark the beginning or end of a ceremony or ritual. Ringing a bell throughout a space or home clears the energy and provides protection. Chimes hung near doors or windows will clear the energy as well as protect and elevate the environment by attracting harmonious vibrations. Witch bells hung on the front door repel unwelcomed energy.

Chanting

Description

Chanting is a practice similar to singing, except instead of using your full vocal range, you use a limited range of notes or just one note. Chanting is common in religious traditions as well as in spiritual practices such as yoga and meditation. Chants are also used in recreational settings, such as sports events and music performances. The word *chant* comes from the Latin *cantare*, meaning "to sing."

History and Lore

Although the exact origin of the practice of chanting is unknown, it has long been a prominent part of many of the world's most ancient religions, including Buddhism, Christianity, Hinduism, Islam, and Judaism. In Buddhism, chanting is a way of preparing the mind for meditation. Gregorian chant, named for Pope Gregory I (c. 540–604) and traditionally sung by church choirs, is practiced in the Roman Catholic religion. Both Hinduism and Islam include the practice of chanting mantras (see entry in this chapter). In Judaism, portions of the Torah are often chanted during services.

Uses

Chanting works with the throat chakra to release any energy blockages and is known to boost immune function due to its ability to strengthen the muscles responsible for respiratory function. In meditation, chanting turns the mind inward and allows you to focus on the sound of your voice and your breath and begin a process of self-observation and discovery. Chant at the beginning of a yoga class to prepare your mind for what you're about to experience and to stay present in your body. The vibration and sound of chanting can also help you push through mental, emotional, or physical barriers. It is thought to stimulate cellular energy, assisting in harmonizing the energy field. Chanting may regulate brain-wave patterns into alpha or beta states, allowing for relaxation and deeper meditation. When chanting in a group, you'll find that the practice serves to unite those present and create a feeling of "oneness."

Drum

Description

A drum is a percussion instrument consisting of a hollow cylindrical shell with a membrane (also called a drumhead or drum skin) stretched over one or both ends. A sound is produced when the membrane is struck with the hand, a stick, a mallet, or another implement. The word *drum* is most likely of imitative origin, or onomatopoeia, meaning that the sound of the word is meant to imitate the sound associated with the object. Drums have many musical, ceremonial, spiritual, and military applications.

History and Lore

The drum is one of the world's oldest musical instruments, dating back to 6000 B.C.E. in Mesopotamia. The ancient Greeks and Romans used a shallow circular drum called a tympanum in worship ceremonies. The "talking drum" of West Africa, whose tone can be regulated to mimic human speech, has been in use for 2,500 years. The drum kit—a collection of multiple drums played together—first appeared toward the end of the nineteenth century. Throughout history, drums have been used for military purposes, such as to rally troops or intimidate the enemy.

Uses

Consider incorporating drums into your spiritual practices. For example, shamanic drumming induces a trance-like state with the purpose of connecting with the spiritual dimension of existence. It typically starts out with a slow rhythm that steadily increases and then slows again at the end of the session. Different rhythms are believed to activate various states of healing. Slower, steadier rhythms provide grounding energy, while heartbeat-style rhythms promote self-love and assist with emotional healing. The connection to the beat of the drum allows for brain-wave entrainment, or synchronization, allowing the mind to enter a state of deep relaxation. Try listening to a recording of drums during meditation, or perhaps join a local drum circle to get in on the action and experience the unifying powers of this ancient instrument.

Flute

Description

A flute is a high-pitched woodwind instrument that consists of
a slender tube that is closed at one end and has keys and finger holes
on one side. Sound is produced when breath is blown into an opening near the
closed end. The oldest known flutes are made of bone or ivory; more modern
flutes are made of wood or metal. A person who plays the flute is called a flautist.

History and Lore

Discovered in caves in southwestern Germany, the world's oldest known musical
instruments are flutes that are estimated to be between 42,000 and 43,000 years
old. Flutes have been central to Indian classical music since 1500 B.C.E. The Hindu
deity Krishna is typically depicted playing the flute. The German inventor and
musician Theobald Boehm (1794–1881) is essentially responsible for the flute as
we know it today. His system of flute keywork is known as the Boehm system.
Native Americans have a long history of using the flute for communication with
the spiritual world.

Uses

Flute music is considered very relaxing, which makes it a popular choice for
meditation and other spiritual practices. Flute music is especially conducive to
exploring and releasing emotions. It is believed to have a profound ability to assist
with connecting to the higher self while promoting spiritual awareness. Playing
these soft sounds in a daily ritual allows for emotional cleansing and clarity of mind.
Listening to flute music is also thought to awaken dormant spiritual connections,
and aid in self-transformation. Flute music is wonderful for meditation, particularly
Zen Buddhist meditation, as it produces a deep sense of inner calm and well-being.
Chinese bamboo flute music is another great option to support your spiritual practice.
If you play the flute yourself, the focus on breathwork is actually quite meditative (see
the Breathwork entry in Chapter 9).

Gong

Description

A gong is a musical instrument that consists of a metal (usually bronze) disk that makes a loud, resonant sound when struck with a padded mallet or hammer. The disk generally has a rim and either is flat or has a raised knob called a "boss" or "nipple" in the center. Gongs are usually suspended vertically from a cord, although there are also gongs that are played horizontally, such as bowl gongs.

History and Lore

The gong originated in China and later spread to Southeast Asia and Africa. Ancient gongs had many uses, including calling workers in from the fields, announcing military presence, and aiding in meditation and ceremonial practices. Gongs are prominently featured in gamelans, which are Indonesian orchestras composed entirely of percussion instruments. Sculptural gongs serve as both a musical instrument and a piece of art.

Uses

One very popular energy healing practice is the gong bath. This is a form of sound therapy in which a gong master plays a gong in the center of a room while "bathers" lie on the ground around the gong and soak up the sound and vibration, promoting deep relaxation and emotional release. It's best to do this in a private or group setting with an actual gong so you can best feel its power, but you can also try it at home with recorded gong sounds. The sound of a gong can also add a new dimension to meditation and other spiritual practices. The tone keeps your mind focused in the present and, depending on the size of the gong, the vibration can sometimes be felt physically, bringing awareness back to your body.

Hz Frequencies

Description

The foundation of any sound can be chronicled by a unit of measurement known as the hertz (Hz), which is equal to one cycle per second. For example, a tone of 285 Hz vibrates 285 times per second. In more complex sound combinations, frequencies may be intertwined and adjusted according to timbre and harmony.

History and Lore

The German physicist Heinrich Rudolf Hertz (1857–1894) is credited with proving the existence of electromagnetic waves previously predicted by James Clerk Maxwell's equations of electromagnetism. Hertz's experiments described what we now know as radio waves, and measured the waves' oscillations per second; because of his work, the unit of measurement of these frequencies was named in his honor. The hertz as a unit of frequency is now known universally across various fields of study, from telecommunications to astronomy. Today, musicians and audio engineers use hertz to tune instruments and control sound quality.

Uses

Within the realm of energy healing, Hz frequencies are associated with tuning the physical body into the spiritual realms. They are thought to induce healing, invite spiritual awakening, forge a connection to the universe, and facilitate communication with angelic realms. Listening to the frequency 396 Hz, for example, targets imbalances in the root chakra, while 1,152 Hz may provide spiritual purification from negative energies within the body. Listening to frequencies that align with your energy healing needs while meditating, sleeping, or simply as background noise is believed to yield the best results with long-term practice.

Mantra

Description

A mantra is a sound, word, or phrase that is repeated mentally or aloud as part of a spiritual or other practice. It is believed that the use of a mantra can have a powerful or even life-changing effect. In Hinduism, mantras are considered sacred. The word *mantra* comes from the Sanskrit words *manas*, meaning "mind," and *tra*, meaning "tool."

History and Lore

Mantras are a major component of the Vedas, a body of ancient Indian texts composed in Sanskrit. Dating back to roughly 1500 B.C.E., the Vedas are the oldest Hindu texts and among the oldest sacred texts in the world. In Hinduism, mantras accompany ritual acts. In Buddhism, mantras are chanted in meditation and to achieve enlightenment. Perhaps the simplest and best-known mantra is "Om," which is known as the "Pranava Mantra," or the supreme mantra. (In Sanskrit, *prana* means "life force.") Many yoga classes open and close with the chanting of this mantra.

Uses

A mantra can serve various purposes in your spiritual practice. The repetitive phrases can aid concentration and shift your vibration to one of a higher consciousness. Starting off a meditation or yoga session with the chanting of a mantra can help you state your intention for the session and keep your mind focused throughout. You might also choose to use a motivational mantra for times during your practice when your energy feels stuck or uninspired. Even something as simple as "I can do this" can help reset your energy. A mantra can also be a sort of prayer—to a deity, nature, the universe, or yourself. You can use an established Hindu, Buddhist, or other mantra, or you can make up your own.

Rattle

Description

A rattle is a hollow percussion instrument that makes a sound when shaken. It can be made of almost any material and contains tiny items such as seeds, beans, or pebbles that make the rattling sound. The word *rattle* is most likely of imitative origin, or onomatopoeia, meaning that the sound of the word is meant to imitate the sound associated with the object. Etymologically, it comes from the Old English *hratele*, a kind of plant with rattling seed capsules.

History and Lore

The rattle is one of the oldest musical instruments. It comes in many different forms, from the maraca, a Latin American instrument that consists of a dried hollow gourd traditionally played in pairs, to the egg shaker, which is small and egg-shaped. Native Americans use wood, rawhide, gourds, and other materials to make rattles used in tribal dances and ceremonies. Shamans of northern Asia and North and South America use rattles for healing, divination, and communication with spirits.

Uses

The principal use of a rattle is for clearing and balancing your energy field. The vibrations produced by the rattle break up stagnant and negative energies. Moving the rattle in circular or figure-eight motions over your seven chakras aids in the healing and balancing of your vibrational force. In meditation, the sound of a rattle has a similar effect to that of a drum or a gong (see entries in this chapter): It focuses your attention and keeps you grounded in the present moment. You might also try using a rattle in the shamanic tradition of calling upon spiritual forces for aid during a struggle.

Singing Bowl

Description

A singing bowl is a percussion instrument that is actually a type of standing bell. The bowl produces a sound when struck with a mallet or other implement, or when the implement is rubbed along the rim of the bowl. The resonant sound is reminiscent of singing, hence the name. Singing bowls are most often metal, usually a copper-heavy alloy, but may also be made of quartz crystal.

History and Lore

The singing bowl originated in Himalayan regions and is now used worldwide. Traditionally, singing bowls were made of a combination of seven metals, corresponding to the seven "planets" that were known at the time: gold (the sun), silver (the moon), copper (Venus), iron (Mars), tin (Jupiter), mercury/quicksilver (Mercury), and lead (Saturn). There is also a connection to the seven chakras, or energy centers, of the body. In some Buddhist practices, the sound of the singing bowl signals the beginning and end of a period of silent meditation. In Japan, singing bowls are used in funeral ceremonies.

Uses

Singing bowls are used in many spiritual and holistic health traditions for relaxation, meditation, and healing. They clear negativity to create a space conducive for deep healing, and they are thought to balance the chakras and aid in stress relief. You can also meditate on the sound of the bowl itself or you can use the sound as a way to focus your attention on the present moment. The vibrations of the bowl interact with your brain waves, allowing for deeper connection in spiritual work. The singing bowl is sometimes used at the end of a yoga practice during Shavasana, or Corpse Pose, to aid in relaxation following a strenuous session.

Sound Baths

Description

A sound bath is an immersive experience whereby participants become enveloped in the calming sounds of specific instruments, such as singing bowls, gongs, and rattles. The purpose of this practice is to support a relaxing, meditative state designed for stress relief and mind-body connection.

History and Lore

The modern-day idea of a sound bath evolved from the ancient practice of sound healing (see entry in this chapter). In the 1960s and 1970s, many musicians partnered with sound healers to experiment with effects of immersing participants in music. In 1975, Don Conreaux, a musician and sound healer, hosted the first sound bath in San Francisco. He used gongs and other instruments to create a hypnotic and mesmerizing sound experience for participants wishing to be transported via music to a meditative state.

Uses

In energy healing, sound baths help clear emotional and spiritual blockages. Sound baths are often group experiences, conducted either outdoors or in enclosed spaces. The primary goal of the sound bath is to calm the mind and body, with a strong focus on relaxation. Participants simply lie in a comfortable position and absorb the sounds, allowing the music and vibrations to flood the senses. The instruments send waves of sound through the body, assisting with the restoration of energetic balance and natural rhythm, beneficial sleep, and mental clarity. Additionally, sound baths are excellent ways to connect with your community and feel the benefits of positive social interactions.

Sound Healing

Description

Sound healing is a therapeutic energy healing practice that uses sound frequencies to heal the physical, mental, and emotional body. It is primarily used to target a specific imbalance in the body and is personalized to the participant. The goal is to restore harmony within the body so as to facilitate a conducive environment for faster healing.

History and Lore

The practice of healing through sound dates back to most ancient civilizations, including in Greece, Egypt, and India. These societies believed that sound carries transformative power and that methods such as singing bowls, chanting, and chimes would encourage the body to heal itself. The Swiss scientist and philosopher Hans Jenny (1904–1972) is credited with bringing the practice of sound healing to modern times. In the mid-twentieth century, he conducted research that helped reveal the effects of sound waves, leading to the development of sound therapy in modern medicine and technologies such as ultrasound and sonography.

Uses

Sound therapy is usually conducted in a private session that is personalized for the participant and has a specific goal. You may find it beneficial to seek out a sound therapist near you or you may want to begin to experiment on your own. Either way, it's best to first set an intention, such as energy balancing, relaxation, emotional release, or stress management, then listen to different sounds to see what addresses your needs. You can use any type of sound that works for you—what's most important is your response and receptiveness. The feeling of release, euphoria, or intense emotion signifies your body is receptive to the healing the sounds provide as they vibrate through the cells of your body to restore and heal.

7

The Power of
Divination Systems

Whether you're seeking answers to specific questions or searching for a deeper connection to the universe, divination systems, tools, and practices can be incredibly valuable. Divination is the practice of discovering the hidden significance or cause of events. The divination items and practices in this book have a wide range of uses and applications, and come from cultural traditions that may have originated thousands of years and thousands of miles apart. In fact, they have been present in nearly all civilizations, both ancient and modern. But what they all have in common is a connection to something outside the realm of the visible world. Tapping into the unseen energies of the universe requires an open mind, an open heart, and a sense of adventure, and nowhere is this more important than in the area of divination.

Divination is a direct connection with the forces that surround and affect us. Aligning your energy field to confer with the unseen realms is a deeply profound process—one that requires great energetic awareness and health. Divination brings information from the beyond into your own energetic field in order to fulfill your life purpose, heal your energy, and find greater peace.

From searching the stars for information about the events in our lives (astrology) to searching our dreams for important messages (dream interpretation), the topics covered in this chapter add a new dimension to your daily life and show you that perhaps there's more to life than meets the eye. Divination tools, systems, and practices are a way to gain insight, clarity, and guidance on important life path decisions. These tools are ways you can illuminate your own inner wisdom, amplifying its power and assisting your personal strength. They all require a dedication to seeing beyond your physical sight and instead using your inner wisdom.

Certain tools and practices listed in this chapter will likely appeal to your curiosity more than others. Whether you are drawn to tarot readings, numerology, or astral projection, you'll be gaining a deeper understanding of your energy healing journey. Offering support and inspiration, these divination practices will not just unlock your existing connection to the spiritual realms, but will also connect you to the magic of the universe itself.

Akashic Records

Description

The Akashic records are a cosmic library—a database full of information about all souls' journeys in past, present, and future lifetimes. They are a repository of collective information, where every soul's imprint, spoken word, thought, and action has contributed to a universally accessible record. Originating in ancient spiritual traditions of Hinduism, the term *Akasha* in Sanskrit means "cosmic space" or "astral light." When pondering the trajectories upon which every choice can lead you, consulting your Akashic records is considered a way in which to access clear insight.

History and Lore

Although referenced in Hinduism, Buddhism, ancient Egypt, and ancient Greece, this belief in collective wisdom was brought to modern understanding through the work of Helena Blavatsky in the late nineteenth century. She described the records as a collective memory humans are able to access through spiritual methods. Now the Akashic records are understood through a lens of theosophy, which is a spiritual movement calling back to ancient religions with an understanding that all souls are connected.

Uses

The Akashic records can be accessed by yourself, and also by practitioners with your permission simply by giving them your name. If you are feeling stagnant or stuck, particularly with questions of life purpose and path, the Akashic records are helpful tools of insight and clarity. Accessing the records is a helpful way to clear blockages and rebalance your energy flow, as they assist in finding less obvious root causes of energy imbalances. The can even provide resolutions to issues causing energetic imbalance, such as karmic lessons and past-life traumas. From a trance-like or meditative state, you may enter these records and communicate with the keepers, who are spiritual guides whose job is to manage your records. Going in with a focused intention will assist you in asking the correct questions to get you the information needed. Answers may come immediately, or in the days following your session in dreams, symbols, or synchronistic anomalies.

Astral Projection

Description

Astral projection, or astral travel, is a type of out-of-body experience in which the astral body leaves the physical body and travels in a separate dimension known as the astral plane or spirit world. The astral body is a supersensible body, meaning it is beyond or above perception by the physical senses. Many people believe there is a silver cord that connects the two bodies during astral projection, which allows the traveler to return to their physical body when the experience ends. Some believe that dreaming is a form of astral projection.

History and Lore

The exact origins of the practice of astral projection are unknown. What is clear, though, is that the idea of astral travel is rooted in the ancient religious belief in an afterlife. In many religions, it is believed that when the physical body dies, the spirit or soul continues on or ascends to a higher realm. The ancient Egyptians believed the soul had the ability to hover outside the physical body. The ancient Indian religions of Hinduism and Buddhism include a belief in reincarnation, which is the rebirth of the soul (or spirit or consciousness) in another body after death.

Uses

In the world of energy healing, it is generally believed that astral projection is a skill you can learn; it simply takes practice. Most astral travel practices look a lot like meditation: You find a comfortable position in a quiet place, close your eyes, and achieve a state of complete relaxation and focus. From there, your mind does the work of moving your soul from your body. Astral traveling allows for access to an abundant energy that you can channel for your own healing. Fostering a connection with the astral body and the energies available there facilitates a sense of well-being, mindfulness, and peace. Astral projection is also a way of getting in touch with your nonphysical self and learning about who you are on the deepest level. It is believed to be a way to communicate with your own higher consciousness as well as high-vibrational energetic beings in other realms, such as angels and guardians. It also delivers a unique perspective, giving clarity to choices and life purpose decisions you have to make on the earthly plane. It can assist with past-life recall and provides an overall more powerful meditation experience. Regularly working on astral projection also increases intuition and psychic awareness.

Astrology

Description

Astrology is the study of the sun, moon, stars, and planets based on the premise that there is a connection between these celestial bodies and the events that happen here on earth. A major component of astrology is the zodiac—the band of sky demarcated by the path the sun takes as it travels around the earth over the course of a year. In Western astrology, the twelve signs of the zodiac—Aries, Taurus, Gemini, Cancer, Leo, Virgo, Libra, Scorpio, Sagittarius, Capricorn, Aquarius, and Pisces—are used to generate a horoscope, a forecast of a person's future based on the position of the stars and planets on a given day, usually the person's birthday. But there are many other forms of astrology, some going back thousands of years. Chinese astrology also includes a zodiac that is divided into twelve parts, but in this case it represents twelve years, not twelve months. Each year in the Chinese zodiac is represented by a different animal. Vedic astrology is the traditional Hindu system of astrology. Its Indian name, *Jyotish*, means "science of light," referring to the idea that the celestial bodies shine their light and energy upon the earth.

History and Lore

The Babylonians are generally credited with the creation of astrology—although it's believed that they adopted the idea of the zodiac from the ancient Egyptians. Early on, astrology was largely used to predict weather patterns for agricultural purposes, but over time the practice broadened to include forecasting natural disasters, war, and other events that affected human life. Greek philosophers such as Plato and Aristotle studied astrology and contributed to it being considered a science. However, the two related fields of astrology and astronomy eventually diverged, and today astrology is generally considered an esoteric practice.

Uses

There are many ways to incorporate astrology into your energy healing practice. The horoscopes you find online can be fun to read, but they're not always based on true astrology. The study of astrology is vast, and best begins with finding a trusted practitioner or embarking on your own journey with comprehensive books. A good first step is to begin by getting a copy of your birth chart, which is a diagram showing the positions of celestial bodies at the moment of your birth. Tuning your energy to that of the planetary systems and seasons increases its influence in other energy healing modalities. For example, utilizing crystals that correspond to zodiac signs balances the energy field, and scheduling rituals that align with the moon's phases allows for deeper connection between the self and the universe. Astrology can also shed light upon your life purpose, assist you with personal development, and provide clarity with life decisions as they present themselves. Modern astrology is less about fortune-telling and more about being a beneficial tool for revealing destructive personal patterns and supporting a reliable inner wisdom.

Aura Reading

Description

An aura is a field of energy surrounding a person or object. Your aura is unique to you, but there are eight aura colors. Most people have a combination of two. Around people, they are thought of as an energy signature, which could be considered a personality type, but acting on a much deeper, soulful level. They represent the authentic vibrational waves a person emits. Some believe that the ability to see auras can be learned and honed with practice; others believe that only certain people are endowed with this skill or "gift." In an aura reading, a psychic, healer, or other specialist examines your aura for information about your thoughts, feelings, and other personal attributes. Sometimes auras appear as layers of colored light surrounding a person. Other times auras are invisible but can still be sensed or perceived by the specialist. The word *aura* comes from the Greek *aura*, meaning "breath."

History and Lore

The concept of auras is ancient and is found in many spiritual traditions. In the Bible, references to light surrounding certain figures are often interpreted as references to auras. Many depictions of Jesus, Mary, and other biblical figures include shining halos or radiant layers of light surrounding their bodies. In Hinduism, the colors of a person's aura are considered to be kundalini energy, which resides at the base of the spine until it is activated (through practices such as yoga) and propelled upward through the chakras. The colors of the Buddhist flag (blue, yellow, red, white, and orange) represent the colors of the aura that surrounded the Buddha when he achieved enlightenment.

Uses

Knowing your aura can help you understand yourself. It can be a challenge understanding your own wants, needs, and direction in this lifetime. Auras don't just show you who you authentically are; they reveal what energies you may require to feel more comfortable in your life. Understanding your aura can help you live life more authentically in every facet of life—career, relationship to self, money, working out, motivation, relationships, and even your personal style. Find a well-respected aura reader in your area or solicit a suggestion from someone you trust. Learning more about the auras can help you decipher them as well. Every color has a specific energetic vibration, and everyone is able to pick up on those distinct vibrations, even if they aren't able to see them. A good time to get an aura reading is when you are at a crossroads in your life, are uncertain about your feelings on a certain matter, or have questions about something you're experiencing. Some aura readers will discuss your past and future as well as your present, while others will only evaluate your aura in the present moment.

Ayahuasca

Description

The hallucinogenic drink called ayahuasca is made from the bark and stem of the tropical vine (*Banisteriopsis caapi*) with the leaves of the chacruna plant (*Psychotria viridis*). It was created by the Indigenous South Americans of the Amazon rainforest basin, but it is now found around the world. Ayahuasca is valued for its claimed healing, visionary, and revelatory powers.

History and Lore

While Peru has become most associated with the production of ayahuasca, it has been found integrated in different ways in a multitude of tribes within the countries through which the Amazon rainforest stretches, such as Brazil, Colombia, Ecuador, Venezuela, and Bolivia. Plant-derived psychoactive drugs played a significant role in Indigenous South American religions for thousands of years, but the English botanist Richard Spruce introduced these plants to a wider audience after encountering them in 1851. Ayahuasca contains DMT, or N,N-Dimethyltryptamine, a hallucinogenic tryptamine drug that naturally occurs in many plant species and is illegal in many countries, including the United States. The influx of tourists seeking to consume the ayahuasca mixture surged in Peru in the late twentieth century. Batches of this drink are prepared by a shaman (or ayahuascero) and taken by participants in groups. Nausea, vomiting, and other digestive issues are a common side effect.

Uses

Those who participate in these ceremonial traditions do so to experience a deep cleansing of a physical, emotional, and spiritual nature. Many swear by ayahuasca as a pivotal part of deep emotional healing from a variety of mental health, addiction, and trauma-induced issues. It is said to elevate consciousness and bring clarity of mind to the participant. It is important to note that there are severe health risks involved with taking this drug, including psychosis, strokes, and even death.

Channeling

Description

Channeling, or mediumship, is the practice of serving as a medium through which a spirit communicates with a living person. This can take two forms: In the first, the medium serves as the middleperson in a conversation between a spirit and a client (often a personal friend or family member of the departed). In the second, the medium goes into a trance wherein he or she vacates his or her physical body and allows the spirit to use it to communicate directly with the client. In the latter case, the medium may not be aware of the conversation taking place.

History and Lore

Attempting to communicate with the dead is an ancient practice found in many cultures. Shamans and witch doctors traditionally contacted the spirits. Channeling gained widespread popularity through the rise of Spiritualism, a nineteenth-century religious movement in the United States and the United Kingdom. Spiritualism is based on the beliefs that the spirits of the dead both desire and are able to communicate with the living, that spirits are more advanced than the living, and that spirits can give the living useful knowledge.

Uses

Channeling a loved one is usually done via patience, practice, and emotion. The bridge between worlds is easiest felt through feelings, especially when remembering a memorable time or a joyful moment shared. Many also find that channeling sessions bring healing to the participants' energy fields, as the experience unites souls and thins the veil between realms. When the emotions are too strong to siphon through yourself, contact a trusted medium. In a channeling session either by yourself or with a medium, you may feel intense emotions, flashes of memory, and sudden insight, as well as a sense of peace, connection, and closure. Channeling should always be a calming and healing experience, never fearful or anxiety-producing.

Dream Interpretation/ Dream Journal

Description

When our bodies go to sleep at night, our minds remain active, producing dreams—whether we remember them or not. Some dreams are bizarre and otherworldly, and others feel so real that we're surprised (and often relieved) when we wake up. Dream interpretation is the practice of assigning meaning to these dreams, which you can then apply to your life in different ways. A dream journal is a tool used for interpreting dreams; in it you record specific images or situations found in your dreams, summarize any details that stand out, and explore emotions felt.

History and Lore

Humans have always been fascinated by dreams. The ancient Egyptians believed that dreams were a means of divine intervention and had priests interpret their messages. The ancient Greeks took dreams to be omens of things to come. The Austrian neurologist and father of psychoanalysis Sigmund Freud (1856–1939) asserted that dreams are a form of wish fulfillment—subconscious attempts to solve conflicts and act out our deepest impulses. In his book *The Interpretation of Dreams*, Freud wrote that the messages in dreams are disguised in order to get them past the "censor" of the preconscious; thus, dreams have to be decoded or interpreted for their true meanings. The Swiss psychotherapist Carl Jung (1875–1961) took Freud's theory one step further and proposed two approaches to interpreting dreams: the objective and the subjective. In the objective approach, the people in a dream represent who they actually are: Your mother is your mother, your father is your father, etc. In the subjective approach, each person in a dream represents some part of yourself: For example, if there is a mother in a dream, that person represents the maternal aspects of the dreamer.

Uses

Interpreting your dreams can be fun and enlightening. The insights that elude us in our waking minds are the first to find us in the dream state. These often shrugged-off symbols can be catalysts for deep energetic healing with the appropriate attention given. The first step is to record your dreams in detail so that you don't forget them. Keeping a dream journal is a great way to do this. If you prefer to keep a digital dream journal instead of a paper one, there are several apps that you can use to record your dreams using your smartphone, tablet, or computer. You might also consider using an audio recording device to narrate and record your dreams orally. Additionally, you can consult a dream dictionary (there are many available online) or a dream interpreter to discover the meaning behind a given dream. Depending on the resource or person you consult, you may get either a vague or specific interpretation. For example, falling in a dream may represent general fears or anxieties about something in your life, or it may mean that a specific part of your life—your job, your relationship—is rapidly moving in the wrong direction. Mindfully noting these symbols may break apart subconscious blocks, allowing for energy healing to accelerate.

ESP

Description

ESP, which stands for extrasensory perception, is the ability to receive information using the mind rather than the five physical senses (sight, hearing, smell, taste, and touch). It is also known as the sixth sense. There are many types of ESP, including clairvoyance (paranormal seeing), clairaudience (paranormal hearing), and clairsentience (paranormal sensing or feeling). For example, a clairvoyant individual has the ability to "see" events or people that do not exist in the present time, a clairaudient person is able to "hear" past or future events or voices, and a clairsentient person can "feel" the emotions of others.

History and Lore

Beginning in the late 1920s, while employed at the newly founded Duke University, the American botanist J.B. Rhine (1895–1980) and his wife, Louisa, performed research in a field they called "parapsychology," which covers such abilities as telepathy, clairvoyance, and precognition. Parapsychology built on the existing field of "psychical" research, whose main goal was to find evidence of an afterlife. In one of the Rhines' ESP experiments, a "sender" would look at a set of ESP cards bearing a series of symbols, and the "receiver" would say which symbol was on each card. The Rhines' work led to the development of the Duke Parapsychology Laboratory in 1935 and the official recognition of parapsychology as a field of experimental science.

Uses

Exploring your sixth sense opens up a world of seemingly almost superhuman abilities to heal your energy. Rather than being the stuff fiction is made of, ESP actually expands the way in which you typically perceive the world, allowing for better understanding of yourself, your energy, and those around you. It is thought to accelerate learning, improve creativity, and invite more meaningful connection with others. ESP allows you to explore perception outside of the five senses, thus creating pathways to healing and finding solutions to problems in ways that are outside of the box. Focusing on broadening the limits of your natural senses can be done with daily practices such as telepathy exercises with a friend, free writing or drawing, or simple meditation where focus is expanded to include, notice, and document every experience in the present moment. There is an endless array of books, films, websites, and other media that deal with the topic of ESP, allowing anyone to make a hobby out of studying (and even practicing) this fascinating phenomenon.

Human Design

Description

Human Design is a system that blends principles of the I Ching, Kabbalah, astrology, chakras, and even quantum physics to create a window where an individual can perceive their personality, innate strengths, and weaknesses. The system includes four key components: Type, or how a person is designed to interact with the world; Authority, which represents the way someone authentically makes decisions; Profile, a series of numbers describing the individual's life theme and lessons to be learned; and Center, which is concerned with a person's energy dynamics. There are five Types, each with unique characteristics: generators, manifestors, projectors, reflectors, and manifesting generators. Each individual practicing Human Design receives a "chart" by plugging in their birth date, birth time, and birth location.

History and Lore

The founder, Ra Ura Hu, born Robert Alan Krakower (1948–2011) in Montreal, Canada, developed this system after what he considered to be a mystical encounter in 1987. He reported that a "voice" spoke to him for eight days and nights, through which he received teachings and insights about the nature of human consciousness. His experience became the foundation for what we know today as Human Design.

Uses

Human Design is considered a tool for self-discovery, rather than a religion or spiritual practice. Its emphasis is on deconditioning a person from societal programming so they can learn to best implement their personal energy for practical application. The system focuses on the individual's unique energy to achieve true potential and cultivate an ability to self-heal. By aligning specific holistic practices to your energy type, you can address energy healing in nurturing, practical ways. You can use Human Design to integrate ancient wisdom into daily life, making choices that are more authentically aligned to you. You can begin by getting your own Human Design chart from one of the many online generators. Afterward, you may wish to embark upon your own study using the multitude of resources in books and online, or by consulting a trusted Human Design practitioner.

Hypnosis

Description

Hypnosis, also referred to as hypnotherapy, is a state of deep relaxation and focused concentration. It is often used to manage stress, to assist in the disruption of negative habits you wish to end, and as a complementary therapy to medical or psychological treatments and procedures. Usually, a trained hypnotherapist guides the patient through a series of exercises that relax and focus the mind. It is a common misconception that people become unconscious, go to sleep, or lose control under hypnosis. In fact, hypnotherapy allows for a more concerted effort of the mind to make positive changes where the participant is fully in control.

History and Lore

The practice of hypnosis has been found in virtually every culture throughout time. In ancient Egypt, hieroglyphics in tombs believed to be from 3000 B.C.E. depict the use of hypnosis. Ancient Greeks reportedly used hypnotherapy for healing and for medical procedures, including surgery. For centuries it has been a practice of Hindu fakirs (holy men), and Indigenous and shamanic healers. In the eighteenth century, the Austrian physician Franz Anton Mesmer (1734–1815) brought attention to the concept of hypnosis with his theory of energetic transference between individuals, which could be harnessed for healing. Later, in the nineteenth century, the Scottish doctor James Braid (1795–1850) coined the term *hypnotism* to give it further distinction in the medical community, where it was gaining popularity.

Uses

In modern times, the use of hypnotherapy has become a popular way to deal with stress, assist in pain management, as well as recover from physical and psychological trauma. In a focused state of awareness, it becomes easier to access the subconscious mind and to channel energetic healing. In this relaxed state, practitioners can assist with releasing blockages, limiting beliefs, and traumas that hinder the flow of energy in the body. As a low-risk way to manage symptoms of a multitude of conditions, hypnosis is also becoming an increasingly acceptable form of complementary therapy in the medical community. It is especially helpful in rerouting negative behavior patterns related to eating disorders, addictions, and phobias. In a spiritual sense, hypnosis allows for introspection and a deeper connection with higher consciousness. Working with a reputable hypnotherapist will allow you to enter the session with goals aligned to your needs.

I Ching

Description

The I Ching, or Book of Changes, is an ancient Chinese text containing sixty-four interrelated hexagrams originally used for divination, along with commentaries attributed to the Chinese philosopher Confucius (551–479 B.C.E.). The hexagrams represent nature and human endeavor in terms of yin and yang—the seemingly opposing and yet complementary forces of the natural world. The I Ching uses a type of divination called cleromancy, in which an outcome is determined by seemingly random means (such as flipping a coin or rolling a die) but was once believed to reveal the will of God.

History and Lore

The I Ching has evolved over the course of thousands of years. The text originated in an ancient Chinese divination book called the *Zhouyi*, which was assembled between the tenth and the fourth centuries B.C.E. The *Zhouyi* offered a guide to cleromancy using the stalks of the yarrow plant (see entry in Chapter 2), although it is not clear how the stalks translated to the numbers or lines used in the hexagrams. Ultimately, the I Ching evolved into the cosmological text we know today with a series of commentaries known as the "Ten Wings."

Uses

The I Ching still finds relevance in our modern times for its lasting application to personal development and self-reflection, and its explanation of the inner workings of the universe. The I Ching can also be utilized while focusing on the chakras in order to unlock deeper levels of energetic healing. Most of all, it is a philosophical guide to understanding the patterns and complexities of life and your connection to them. Accessing its wisdom to make choices aligned with your life purpose and path allows your energy to align and recenter. If you're new to the I Ching, you may be a bit overwhelmed by the apparent complexity of its ancient methodology. Fortunately, there are many modern interpretations and techniques that simplify the act of consulting the I Ching for guidance and wisdom, one of which is a series of coin tosses you can perform. There are a multitude of online resources with step-by-step instructions for using the I Ching, as well as countless books, classes, and workshops for those interested in this ancient text and its modern applications.

Numerology

Description

Numerology is the study of numbers, their meanings, and their effects on human life. There are many different forms of numerology that originated in cultures all over the world. Gematria, for instance, is a system that assigns numerical value to a word or phrase. An example is the Hebrew word *chai*, meaning "alive," which translates to the number 18, making this a lucky number in Judaism. Birth dates are considered important in numerology, and the "life path" number is the sum of the numbers in a person's date of birth.

History and Lore

Numerology has its roots in ancient Greece and the studies of philosophers and mathematicians such as Pythagoras (c. 570–495 B.C.E.), who believed numbers were the universal language of truth. In the Arabic system of numerology, each letter of the Arabic alphabet has a numerical value. In Chinese numerology, even numbers are considered lucky, due to the belief that good luck comes in pairs.

Uses

Numerology can act as a roadmap to life, enlightening your purpose to humanity as well as assisting with harnessing certain energies to achieve your goals. There is no limit to how deep you can go into the practice of numerology. If you're new to numerology, knowing your "core numbers" is a great place to begin, as they are thought to be the most important. Many websites will generate your core numbers and numerology chart based on the letters of your name and your birth date. You can also calculate your own life path number, the core number thought most influential, by adding up the digits of your birth date. For example, if you were born on October 23, 1972, the equation is $10 + 23 + 1972 = 2005$. Then you add those digits together: $2 + 0 + 0 + 5 = 7$. Once you know your life path number, you can learn about the meanings behind this number. Using your life path number for positive affirmations can align your thoughts with desired outcomes. For example, you would learn that having a life path number 3 reminds you to add creativity to your personal goals. Adding a statement akin to "I express myself with joy and playfulness" to your self-talk can assist in your energy leveling up to meet this vibration. Another fun way to explore numerology is to have your numbers read by a professional numerologist.

Oracle Reading

Description

Oracle readings are used to connect with your personal inner guidance. They are most often conducted through an oracle deck, a set of cards that offers advice and insight into daily life. Their meanings are often flexible and allow for open interpretation through the user. Unlike a tarot deck, an oracle deck can vary in the number of cards as well as the symbols, pictures, and words upon them. Oracle readings have a more flexible structure and a stronger focus on inspiration and reflection than traditional divination readings.

History and Lore

Seeking divine insight through oracles is a practice found in the earliest of human civilizations. The term *oracle* has roots in the Latin verb *orare*, meaning "to pray" or "to speak." The Sumerian and Akkadian cultures of Mesopotamia utilized priests as intermediaries between gods and people, interpreting signs etched on clay tablets. In ancient Egypt, the Book of the Dead details communication rituals between realms via the use of oracles and their insights.

Uses

Consulting an oracle deck when faced with a difficult decision allows for a sense of control and clarity to come over you. Oracle readings support spiritual healing, and encourage personal growth and increased self-awareness. Consulting an oracle deck improves intuition as you focus on goals, challenges, and the emotions that are at the forefront of your mind. Oracle readings also encourage grounding, which is the process of centering yourself in the midst of chaotic feelings and the challenges of life. They are not just for harrowing times—they can also assist with meditation, as they can be used for prompts on what needs to be reflected upon and paid attention to presently.

Palmistry

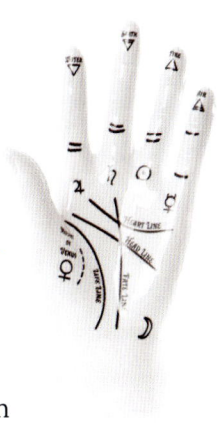

Description

Palmistry, also called palm reading or hand analysis, is the practice of foretelling the future based on the lines, marks, and patterns on the palms of the hands. There are two main approaches to this practice: Chiromancy deals with the lines on the palm, and chirognomy deals with the shape of the hands and the color, shape, and texture of the palm and fingers.

History and Lore

Palmistry is an ancient practice. While the exact timing is unknown, historians believe it originated in India and then spread to China, Egypt, Greece, and eventually Europe. The Greek philosopher Aristotle (384–322 B.C.E.) observed, "Lines are not written into the human hand without reason. They emanate from heavenly influences and man's own individuality." During the Middle Ages, the Catholic Church condemned the practice of palmistry, declaring it a pagan superstition. One of the major figures of palmistry's revival in the nineteenth century was French captain Casimir Stanislas D'Arpentigny (1798–1872), who is credited as the first person to formulate a system of hand-shape classification.

Uses

The curiosity of what those lines on your hands mean is a launching point for self-discovery and reflection. When used as a way to embark upon self-analysis, it can open up pathways for self-understanding. The discovery of patterns and other inherent tendencies provides ways to balance your energy and explore agency in addressing your healing. If you're interested in having your palm read, search for a reputable palm reader in your area. If you're interested in learning the art of palm reading yourself, there are countless resources out there, from books to websites and beyond.

Past-Life Recall

Description

Various cultures believe that the lives we are currently living are not our first—or our last. Hindus and Buddhists, for example, believe in reincarnation, the rebirth of the soul (or spirit or consciousness) in another body after death. Many also believe that it is possible to recall past lives through various practices such as hypnosis and meditation. Past-life recall is the process of remembering those former lives and gleaning information from them that can assist in the present.

History and Lore

The Upanishads, a collection of ancient Sanskrit texts that contributed to the theology of Hinduism, mention both reincarnation and past-life recall, specifically past-life regression, a form of past-life recall using hypnosis. The French psychologist and philosopher (and contemporary of Freud) Pierre Janet (1859–1947) is recognized as one of the first people to make a connection between the events in a person's past life and his or her present-day trauma. Both Janet and Freud experimented with past-life regression as a therapeutic tool. Psychotherapist Brian Weiss (1944–) wrote the influential book *Many Lives, Many Masters* based on his own work using past-life regression to treat his patients. In a *New York Times* article from 2010, Cornell-trained psychiatrist Paul DeBell stated that belief in reincarnation "allows you to experience history as yours. It gives you a different sense of what it means to be human."

Uses

Past-life recall is said to assist with balancing energy, healing trauma, overcoming phobias, and deepening your spiritual connection. You can explore the practice on your own or with the assistance of a hypnotist, therapist, or other specialist. There are also countless books, websites, and other resources that offer information on past-life recall for beginners. As discussed in Chapter 1, amber and opal are two stones that can be used in meditation to help remember past lives. Burning rosemary during meditation or dream work also aids in past-life recall (see Chapter 2).

Pendulum

Description

A pendulum is an item that swings freely from a fixed point under the influence of gravity. Pendulums are known as the timekeeping elements of clocks, but they have many other applications. They are used in religious traditions, divination practices, and spiritual and healing rituals.

History and Lore

The Italian astronomer, physicist, engineer, philosopher, and mathematician Galileo Galilei (1564–1642) became interested in the study of pendulums after observing a swinging chandelier. He went on to make an important discovery about pendulums: The time it takes for a pendulum to complete one swing remains almost exactly the same, regardless of the size of the arc it makes. Building on Galilei's work, the Dutch scientist Christiaan Huygens (1629–1695) built the first pendulum clock in 1656. Censers—incense burners that swing at the end of a chain—appear in various religious and cultural traditions, such as Catholicism.

Uses

Choosing a pendulum is an intuitive process. While pendulums come in a vast array of materials, such as copper for energy amplification or wood for grounding, a popular choice is crystal. Rose quartz, for example, calls in love, while amethyst enhances intuition. Radiesthesia is the use of a pendulum to locate an object or substance or to assess the energy (or "radiation") of a subject. One example of this is dowsing, which utilizes a dowsing object, such as a pendulum, to locate water or minerals underground. You assign meanings to the various movements of the pendulum (for example, swinging from left to right means there is water) and then walk slowly over the search area. Another way to use pendulums is to get answers to questions about your life. You simply "program" the pendulum (deciding which movement means "yes" and which means "no"), and then you ask questions out loud and wait for answers. Pendulums are also used as tools for dowsing in a spiritual sense.

Runes

Description

Runes are the letters of a set of related alphabets used by ancient Germanic peoples prior to the adoption of the Latin alphabet. However, runes were much more than letters as we think of them today: Each rune was a symbol of a principle or power, and it was believed that writing a rune invoked the force it represented. In addition to general writing purposes, runes were used to make calendars, encode secret messages, and cast spells. The word *rune* comes from the Old English *run*, meaning "whisper, talk in secret."

History and Lore

Runes are believed to have derived from one of the many Old Italic alphabets used by the Mediterranean peoples of the first century C.E. The runic alphabets were in use between the third and the thirteenth centuries and were replaced with Latin through the process of Christianization in Europe. The Meldorf brooch (also called the Meldorf fibula) bears what is possibly the oldest known runic inscription. It was discovered in Meldorf, Schleswig-Holstein, Germany, in 1979 and dates back to the mid–first century C.E. However, scholars disagree on whether this inscription is truly runic or proto-runic.

Uses

Like the I Ching or tarot (see entries in this chapter), runes can be used to receive messages and spiritual insight. They are also used as vibrational talismans for energetic healing, as each rune typically represents a natural element, a specific concept, or a spiritual truth. You can visit a rune reader for an experience that is somewhat similar to a tarot card reading, or you can learn how to cast runes and read them yourself. (There are various ways to cast and read runes, all of which vary depending on your questions and your ability to interpret what you uncover. You may roll them or even draw a few individually when starting out.) Begin by reading up on runes and buying a set of your own. They are usually purchased in the form of small tiles or pebbles and may be made of wood, stone, crystal, metal, or even bone. Rune reading is not to be confused with fortune-telling; the runes don't give you direct advice or exact answers. Instead, they offer hints and variables and leave you to work out the details using your intuition.

Scrying Mirror

Description

Scrying is the practice of gleaning information from images "seen" in a reflective, translucent, or luminescent surface. But this is not like looking at your own reflection in the bathroom mirror; instead, the images seen reflect inner spiritual visions. A scrying mirror may be made of a variety of materials, such as crystals, glass, or water. The word *scry* is actually short for *descry*, which means "to catch sight of or detect." *Descry* comes from the Old French *descrier*, meaning "to call, cry out."

History and Lore

Visions received through scrying are thought to come from your own subconscious or higher realms, and throughout time it was commonly believed they came from gods, spirits, or other divine or ethereal influences. The legendary Cup of Jamshid is a famous scrying mirror that appears in Persian mythology. The cup was said to be filled with an elixir of immortality in which the whole world was reflected. The French apothecary and seer Nostradamus (1503–1566) used a bowl of clear water for scrying and then wrote about his visions. Joseph Smith Jr. (1805–1844) founded the Mormon religion based in part on information obtained through the reflections in seer stones.

Uses

Although some firmly believe that only a select few possess scrying abilities, the general consensus is that anyone can learn this ancient art with practice. It enhances intuition and creativity, and improves focus as well. Scrying clears the mind and is believed to cleanse the mind and body of negative energy. The guidance and insight revealed assists with energetic and emotional healing. To begin, purchase a scrying mirror in a store or online, or you can make one yourself. There is a wide variety of options in terms of materials and forms. As you learned in Chapter 1, malachite is a stone that can be used for scrying. You could also try Nostradamus's bowl of water technique, which involves placing a brass scrying bowl full of water on a tripod. Next, you must achieve a meditative or trance-like state that allows for deep inner focus and exploration. Finally, with practice, as you gaze, visions will appear. There are countless resources, including books, websites, and organizations, where you can learn specific scrying methods and how to interpret the visions you see.

Shamanic Journeying

Description

A shaman acts as a medium between the visible physical world (ordinary reality) and the invisible spirit world (non-ordinary reality). Shamans have different roles depending on the culture, but in general they perform healing, divination, and other rituals and practices. A shamanic journey is a process of entering an altered state of consciousness and traveling to the spirit world for any number of reasons—to heal the sick, locate lost souls, or glean information about the future.

History and Lore

Shamanism is an ancient spiritual practice dating back tens of thousands of years. It has existed in many cultures worldwide, from the Mayan and Aztec people of Mexico and Central and South America to the Hmong people of China. The American anthropologist, educator, and author Michael Harner (1929–2018) is a figure in contemporary Western shamanism. He founded the Foundation for Shamanic Studies and wrote the classic book *The Way of the Shaman*.

Uses

In some cultural traditions, a person must be "called" or born into shamanism, or undergo extensive training. Others believe that anyone can contact the spirits while in an altered state of consciousness. Shamanic journeying aims to restore the overall well-being of your spiritual, emotional, and physical health. It is said to invite access to inner wisdom and guidance from spiritual realms. If you're interested in trying shamanic journeying, there are many methods available. One is to listen to a repetitive sound, such as drumming or rattling, to achieve a meditative, trance-like state. Once this state is achieved, your journey may take any number of forms. It may feel like meditation—a deep exploration of your inner self—or you may have the opportunity to communicate with spirits, who could appear to be people or animals. For assistance with your method and interpretation, consult some of the many resources available in print or online (such as the Foundation for Shamanic Studies website, www.shamanism.org), or seek the guidance of a shaman, healer, or other specialist.

Tarot

Description

The tarot is a deck of usually seventy-eight cards that was originally created for card games but now is also used for divination. The deck is divided into two sections: the Major Arcana (twenty-two cards) and the Minor Arcana (fifty-six cards). Each card features a specific concept or archetype—for example, Justice or The Lovers. It is believed that the cards you select can provide answers to questions and show you what you need to see in order to make certain decisions in life.

History and Lore

The tarot (originally known as *trionfi*) originated in the mid-fifteenth century in Europe, where it is still used to play card games. It wasn't until the eighteenth century that tarot card reading first appeared as a divination practice. The French occultist Jean-Baptiste Alliette (1738–1791), also known by the pseudonym Etteilla, is credited with popularizing tarot as a divination method and issuing the first tarot deck created specifically for this purpose.

Uses

Tarot readings can bring clarity to past events for emotional healing and understanding, be tools of divination when unclear which path to take, or even assist in meditation with prompts and insight. Tarot readings can also assist with emotional healing, and certain card spreads, such as the "release spread," support letting go of what no longer serves your energy. Whether you visit a tarot reader or learn to read the cards yourself, this type of reading is very useful for when you need guidance, healing, or desire self-reflection. Once you've had a few tarot card readings, you may feel inspired to buy your own deck and learn how to read the cards yourself. There are endless resources that can help you do this, including online courses, workshops, books, and websites.

Tea Leaves Reading

Description

The reading of tea leaves is also known as tasseography; this word is derived from the French *tasse*, meaning "cup." It is an ancient form of divination that analyzes the patterns found in tea leaves—and sometimes wine sediments or coffee grounds—left in the bottom of a cup after it has been poured out or drunk.

History and Lore

The birthplace of this unique form of fortune-telling is believed to have been in ancient China during the Tang dynasty (618–907 C.E.), when tea drinking became a popular daily ritual for all. Expanding westward trade routes that brought tea also brought the divination practice along with it to Persia (modern-day Iran) and other parts of the Middle East. Blending with existing cultural traditions, tea leaves reading became more than predicting the future—it was also a valued part of storytelling and social gatherings. Eventually, it made its way to Eastern Europe and it flourished within the Romani communities.

Uses

Whether you are looking for guidance, energy healing, or connection to the human experience, tea leaves readings are a unique form of divination. These types of readings are richly layered with variations based on the cultures and the generations of practitioners who added their touches to them. Different teas, for example, are said to yield varying results: Black tea provides excellent leaves for reading, and also a layer of protection for the messages given, while green tea allows for subtle and introspective messages (since it has less of a defined leaf for reading). Creating meaningful rituals by setting intentions and reflecting on messages garnered from tea leaves readings may also release unhealthy patterns and promote energy healing. Some frequently appearing shapes and symbols are universally interpreted—hearts usually signal emotional connections, and birds mean that exciting news is coming to you soon.

8

The Power of Symbols

Symbols are marks or signs that represent ideas, thoughts, or relationships beyond what typical language can communicate. They're abstract thoughts in a visual form. If you've ever held up a heart hand signal to a friend or added an emoji to the end of a text message, you already understand the importance of symbols in everyday life. In the realm of energy healing, symbols hold another essential role: They serve as portals leading us to deeper connection with our own intuition, self, and higher consciousness.

These complex bearers of multilayered meaning appear in almost every area of our lives. From the colors that brighten our world to the numbers and words we use to quantify and communicate, human society functions largely through the use of symbols. The word *symbol* comes from the Greek *sumbolon*, meaning "token for identification."

From the beginning of time as we understand it, symbols have been indispensable components of art, religion, and storytelling. Humans are visual beings, and we respond passionately to imagery in emotional ways. Symbols in nature, in geography, and within different cultures evoke memories and feelings words alone cannot contain. Rituals are special events in which people meaningfully engage with these symbols. These rituals can even be everyday practices in which you can mindfully incorporate significant symbols into your daily life and energy wellness routine.

The subjects in this chapter play important roles in many of the other topics discussed in this book, such as colors and numbers. While reading about the power of stones in Chapter 1, you learned how their color relates to the chakras, or energy centers, of our bodies. You also discovered how numbers are used in studies such as the I Ching and numerology (see entries in Chapter 7). In addition to colors and numbers, in this chapter we'll discuss the importance of shapes, sigils, and words as symbols throughout history and in our modern-day lives. Whether through modern therapeutic practices or ancient traditions, you can harness symbols for insight, wellness, and energy healing.

Amulets

Description

Amulets are either natural or man-made and are believed to hold powers of protection or good fortune for the wearer. An amulet is often carried on the person or kept in a place where its effects are deemed most necessary. The terms *amulet* and *talisman* are sometimes used interchangeably, but a talisman is traditionally defined as an amulet that has been engraved.

History and Lore

One of the oldest known amulets was a bear tooth charm found in the Altai Mountains of Siberia dating back 40,000 years. Prehistoric amulets included those made of animal bones, shells, and clay. In Ancient Egypt, there was no distinction made between magic and medicine, and amulets were part of standard medical practice. In Ancient Greece and Rome, amulets became tools to influence fate and ensure success and prosperity. Medieval European amulets were often merged with Christian symbols and meant to protect against illness and misfortune.

Uses

In modern times, amulets have an important role in signaling cultural identity and heritage, providing a reminder for personal growth, and protecting the wearer. Amulets are often part of personal storytelling, and choosing an amulet that reflects your beliefs encourages a stronger energetic connection and subsequent protection. Creating an amulet that aligns with your own spiritual, emotional, and physical needs can be done with crystals, essential oils, and other materials discussed in this book. Regular cleansing of your amulet ensures its ability to maintain its effectiveness. Ancient charms meant for protection against unseen forces are still popular today, as are individualized creations that reflect your personal aspirations for goals and growth.

Angel Numbers

Description

Angel numbers are numerical sequences that are meant to grab your attention and point you in a new, often realigned, direction in life. Considered messages from angels, or high-vibrational beings from an ethereal realm, they are meant to serve as universal signals to point you toward your purpose. Individual numbers are thought to symbolize specific messages, and different sequences of numbers hold different meanings. For example, 222 signifies a need to trust a life path, and 444 lets you know you're protected.

History and Lore

The origins of angel numbers are intertwined with those of numerology (discussed in Chapter 7). The ancient Greek philosopher Pythagoras laid the foundations for numerology. In the early 20th century, L. Dow Balliett (1847–1929) proposed that every number held its own vibrational frequency, and she is considered a pioneer of modern-style numerology. American author Doreen Virtue (1958–) is credited with coining the term *angel numbers*.

Uses

Angel numbers show up when there are decisions that affect your soul's purpose. When you see an increase in these types of numbers, know that something powerful is happening behind the scenes of the everyday physical world. If you see repeated number sequences, such as 111 or 212, it is possible your angels are trying hard to get your attention. Angel numbers are often referring to what is at the forefront of your mind at this very moment. These messages often offer solutions, life path changes, or support and encourage healing through paying attention to unhealthy life patterns. The numbers work with synchronicity, or repetition past the point where coincidence could explain their appearance. For example, if you see a repeated number pattern on the clock, on a receipt, then on the license plate of the car ahead of you in traffic, it may be time to look into its significance. There are many resources explaining the vibrational frequencies of each number and the meanings they form.

Chakra Balancing

Description

Chakra balancing is a process of balancing and bringing harmony to the energy centers of the body, known as chakras. A variety of methods, such as meditation, visualization, and sound healing, can unblock and cleanse these energy centers. This popular energy healing practice works on the assertion that the body's energy flows through seven chakras, each responsible for a different area of well-being (see the Understanding Chakras section at the beginning of the book).

History and Lore

The ancient Indian texts dating back to 1500 B.C.E. known as the Vedas and the Upanishads reference the concept of energy centers within the body. They describe chakras as being responsible for the flow of energy within the body, as well as the connection to the universe itself. Additionally, chakras are said to be swirling vortexes of energy corresponding to different aspects of a person's life, such as intuition, creativity, and emotions. Balancing these centers can contribute to amplified spiritual growth. In modern times, chakras are widely integrated into a multitude of energy healing practices.

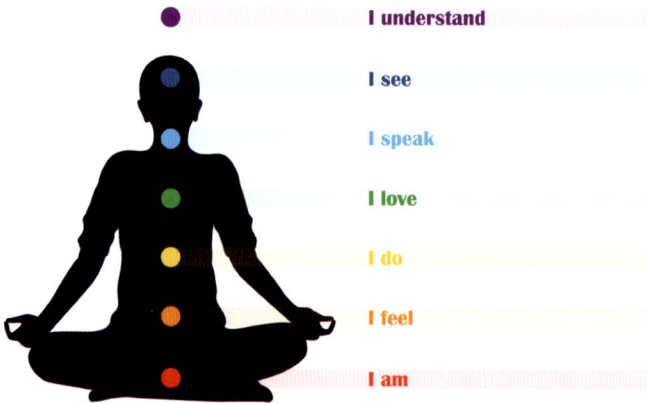

I understand

I see

I speak

I love

I do

I feel

I am

Uses

Chakra balancing incorporates ancient teachings with modern therapeutic techniques to restore harmony within the body, mind, and spirit. Balancing chakras through a variety of methods such as aromatherapy, color healing, crystal healing, or even active meditation can offer an array of emotional, physical, and spiritual benefits. It reduces stress, improves immune function, regulates emotions, and assists with mental clarity. As chakra balancing unblocks the energy centers of the body, it also can result in increased stamina and motivation. This type of chakra work can create deeper spiritual connections to self and allow for healing on a fundamental level. You can embark on this technique with a trusted practitioner or try it on your own with guided meditation and tools discussed in this book.

Colors

Description

What we identify as color is really just the perception by our eyes and brains of the spectrum of light and its interaction with objects and materials. The perception of color also varies by individual and by species. Those who are colorblind lack the ability to see certain colors or to distinguish between colors. As a symbol, color plays a central role in almost everything we do, from "singing the blues" to stopping at red lights.

History and Lore

Humans have always used color as a form of expression, the earliest evidence of which is cave paintings from the Paleolithic era. The ancient Egyptians used color to represent specific characteristics. For instance, Osiris, the god of the afterlife, the underworld, and the dead, is always depicted with green skin—the color of rebirth. Many of the ancient Greek and Roman statues carved in white marble that survive to the present day—such as the Lovatelli Venus from the first century C.E.—once bore bright paint colors that wore off over time. Color also plays an important role in religion. In Christianity, for example, purple is associated with penance and is used during the seasons of Advent and Lent.

There are many fields that feature color symbolism. Color psychology, for instance, is the study of how color affects human behavior. Professionals in this area have shared fascinating findings about the impact of color on our daily lives. For example, the color blue has a calming effect, and in 2000, after the city of Glasgow, Scotland, instituted blue streetlights in certain areas, crime decreased as a result.

Uses

Incorporating colors with a mindful attitude will allow their energies to amplify aspects of your life. Both ancient and modern cultures have recognized the effect colors in decor and design have on mood and mindset. In particular, associating colors with the elements can funnel their power into purpose. For example, green and brown represent earth, and are helpful for promoting abundance and grounding. Placing some green plants around the office or brown vases in your thinking space will provide feelings of calmness and stability. Blue tones resonate with water and invite emotional well-being and adaptability. A few blue crystals can reinforce the color's calming effects. Red or orange call in the element of fire, igniting passion and drive. Throwing some colorful peppers in your dishes or painting an accent wall orange can invigorate your vibe. Get creative with repurposing color as a tool for moving the energy in your life in the directions you'd like it to go.

Cord Removal

Description

Cord removal, which is sometimes referred to as cord cutting, is the releasing of energetic attachments that hinder spiritual and personal growth. It is a practice used when you are feeling particularly weighed down by toxic relationships, environments, or experiences. The idea behind it is that every experience we have—negative, positive, or neutral—creates an unseen energetic cord that links us. If we remove the cord from a negative event, we then have the freedom to move away from the energetic heaviness of that interaction.

History and Lore

Cord removal practices can be found in various ancient cultures and spiritual traditions, where emotional ties were seen as energetic cords of influence. Ancient Egyptians understood the power of severing harmful energetic connections. In Indigenous tribes, shamanic practitioners perform rituals to restore harmony through releasing unnecessary energetic cords. In Buddhism, the idea of detachment, where letting go of unhealthy connections is essential to restoring balance and inner peace, is reminiscent of cord removal.

Uses

The benefits of cord removal are for everyone, but those suffering from trauma or toxic relationships, and even energy healers themselves, may find it especially rewarding. The transformational effects of cord removal allow for emotional freedom and clarity as well as an increased sense of control and safety within personal relationships. Those who find themselves holding onto the feelings, thoughts, and repetitive replays of the past will experience a sense of calmness. Cord removal can be done completely by yourself with visualization and minimal supplies. Finding a quiet space, setting a clear intention, and simply visualizing the cords leaving your body can accomplish the disconnection. You may wish to incorporate meditational music or even some essential oils to assist in your focus during the session.

Sacred Geometry

Description

Geometry is an area of mathematics relating to the relationship of space between lines, curves, points, and surfaces. *Sacred* geometry is the study of the spiritual meaning behind geometrical shapes, patterns, proportions, and forms of the natural world. They are ancient symbols meant to strengthen a spiritual foundation.

History and Lore

Geometry was utilized in many early civilizations and cultures, and appeared as the result of practical needs in building, measuring, and understanding volume. According to the Greek historian and geographer Herodotus (c. 484–425 B.C.E.), it was the ancient Egyptians who established geometry. However, the ancient Mesopotamians also used principles of geometry as did the ancient Chinese and Indians. All of these cultures combined geometric configurations into their sacred architecture and religious art. Structures such as the Great Pyramid of Giza and Stonehenge mirror geometric principles. Celtic art also utilizes lines and spirals, representing balance and harmony. Sacred geometry serves not only as a tool for design, but also as a symbol of our connection to the universe itself.

Uses

The foundational geometric shapes of our natural world hold great spiritual significance. Studying the design of a spider's web, the spiral of a nautilus shell, or the ellipse of an egg are all ways you are observing and responding to visual patterns of energy manifesting in our physical world. Much more than just an aesthetic, incorporating them into your everyday meditations and environments is believed to raise your energetic vibration as well. Mindfully sketching a snowflake or arranging your crystals into a grid resembling a circle, triangle, or the more detailed loops of the "seed of life" shape may give way to insight and inspiration from higher realms.

Shapes

Description

Shapes are fundamental to the way we see and interpret the world around us. From simple geometric shapes such as the circle and the square to more elaborate shapes like the triskelion—an ancient symbol consisting of three bent or curved lines radiating from a common center—shapes carry profound meanings in various religious and cultural traditions as well as energy healing practices. The word *shape* comes from the Old English *gesceap*, meaning "a creation."

History and Lore

The origins of geometry, the branch of mathematics concerned with the shape, size, and relative position of figures, can be traced to ancient Mesopotamia and Egypt around 2000 B.C.E. The ancient Greek mathematician Euclid (birth and death dates unknown, though he was known to be active around 300 B.C.E.) is considered the father of geometry. Platonic solids are three-dimensional polyhedra named for the ancient Greek philosopher and mathematician Plato (c. 428–348 B.C.E.), who theorized that the "classical elements," an early term for the states of matter, were made of these solids.

Uses

Geometric patterns are believed to hold powerful healing properties through their connection to the natural world. As discussed earlier in this chapter, sacred geometry is the study behind the spiritual meaning of shapes and how they bridge our connection to the divine. Energy healers often use patterns and shapes to create harmonic resonance within the body, which in turn promotes balance and healing. Cube-shaped crystals, for example, promote grounding in meditation, while crystals shaped as pyramids amplify intentions for manifestation. Worn as jewelry, spiral shapes are believed to support transformation. Even the chakras are thought to correlate to specific platonic solids: The sphere is associated with the crown chakra and elevates consciousness, while the dodecahedron is associated with the third eye chakra, connecting your vibration to clarity and psychic abilities.

Sigils

Description

The basic definition of a sigil is a seal, such as one used with melted wax to seal an envelope. However, in the energy healing sense, a sigil is an image that acts as a symbolic representation of a desire or the outcome of an intention. The word *sigil* comes from the Latin *signum*, meaning "sign."

History and Lore

In medieval ceremonial magic, the term *sigil* referred to occult signs representing angels and demons that could be summoned through the practice of magic. These sigils were considered equivalent to the names of these beings and therefore gave the magician a certain amount of control over them. One method of creating these sigils was to convert the names of the angels and demons to numbers, which were then incorporated into "magic squares" (arrangements of numbers in square grids where each number is used only once, and each row, column, and diagonal adds up to the same number). When lines were drawn between the numbers, an abstract figure appeared.

Uses

Anyone can create a sigil and use it in a ritual with the goal of manifesting a desire and shifting energy. The resulting symbol you'll create will become the physical representation of your intention. Here's a simple process you can follow:

- Write a simple sentence in all capital letters using the present tense that embodies your desire as if it were already a fact. For example, instead of writing "I WANT TO BE HAPPY," write, "I AM HAPPY."
- Cross out any duplicate letters and rewrite the letters that remain: "I A M H P Y."
- Choose how you will incorporate these letters into a symbol. Some easy options are to use the letters themselves to create an image, or to convert the letters to numbers or Roman numerals based on their positions in the alphabet. For example, "I" is 9 or IX, "A" is 1 or I, and so on.

Once you have created your sigil, you can incorporate it into the ritual or practice of your choice, such as carrying it with you, or making it part of your sacred space or meditation.

Words

Description

Words are the smallest meaningful units of language that can stand on their own. We use words in both written and spoken form to express ourselves, to communicate with one another, and to document our experiences. Unlike some of the other topics in this chapter, words' entire purpose is to represent something else—an idea, an object, an emotion, a sound. In energy healing, words hold vibrations that are uniquely able to influence your energy healing.

History and Lore

Etymology is the branch of linguistics that deals with the history of words, their origins, and how their forms and meanings have changed over time. The word *etymology* comes from the Greek *etumologia*: *etumon*, meaning "true sense of a word," plus *logia*, from *logos*, meaning "one who deals with." It is believed that written language began around 3200 B.C.E. in Mesopotamia.

Uses

Words are central to many energy healing and spiritual practices. Chanting and mantra, covered in Chapter 6, are two examples of ways you can harness the power of words. Another practice, called "imprinting water," combines words and water to create a homeopathic remedy for dealing with emotional issues, energy blockages, or trauma. The idea behind this practice is that words have their own vibrations and water can be imprinted with these vibrations. One way to imprint water is to write a word, such as *love*, on a piece of paper, tape it to the outside of a glass bottle, and then fill the bottle with water. It is then your choice how you use the water: for drinking, for watering plants, for cooking, etc. It is believed that the energy from the word (and your intention in choosing that word) will then be incorporated in the water's use.

9

The Power of Movement

Do you notice you tend to think better if you go for a walk, or that a few deep breaths when you're nervous calms you down? Your body already knows that activity is helpful when you're anxious, nervous, or need to concentrate. While it might seem like the focus of energy healing is often on sitting still and quietly meditating, in this chapter we're going to talk about an equally important aspect of energy healing: movement! Mindfully moving is another technique that you can utilize as a way to unblock, balance, and heal your energy.

Humans are active beings. We run, jump, swim, stretch, dance, play, and perform, all using our unique, amazing bodies. Not only is movement crucial for physical health; it's also essential for mental and emotional well-being. The body has a natural flow of energy, and movement is its way of allowing it to heal, connect, and increase its vitality. In fact, it's more important than ever to take some time each day to put down your phone, step away from your computer, and get mindfully moving.

Throughout this book, we have discussed an essential concept of energy healing: The body can and wants to heal itself. You'll find that movement is integral to that process. Engaging with the body's energy through move-ment increases the body's innate healing capacities. The power of moving promotes wellness and relaxation as well. You'll learn to manage and release negative energy properly and to engage the body's energy points and encourage the flow of positive energy.

The various energy healing practices described in this chapter cover all types of movement, from the subtle but vital act of breathing to the intricate gestures and postures found in practices like qigong and yoga. Some of these, such as dance, may already be very familiar to you, while others, like mudras, may be new. Whether it's finding a local labyrinth to walk or signing up for some tai chi in the park, you are about to learn effective ways to connect with this innate power within. As you discover more about the power of movement, keep an open mind to how your body's energy flow is an essential component in your energy healing journey.

Active Meditation

Description

Meditation is discussed throughout this book as a spiritual practice that involves sitting or standing quietly and focusing your attention inward to achieve a state of calm or to perform deep personal exploration. However, that's not the *only* form meditation can take. Active meditation is a style of meditation that includes physical movements, such as jumping or dancing, followed by silence. The movements allow for both physical and emotional release, while giving the mind a break from thought and worry.

History and Lore

The Indian mystic, guru, and spiritual teacher Osho (1931–1990) created a number of active meditation techniques, which he believed were more applicable to modern life than traditional meditation practices. One such technique is called "dynamic meditation," which involves four stages of movement with music and one stage of silent reflection. Osho's other active meditation methods include kundalini "shaking" meditation, which involves shaking the body and dancing, and nadabrahma "humming" meditation, which involves humming and hand movements. Osho also believed these active meditation techniques served as helpful preparation for more traditional meditation.

Uses

Active meditation has many of the same benefits as standard meditation, plus a few bonus perks. In addition to calming the mind, you also invigorate the body by using your muscles, getting your heart rate up, and boosting blood circulation. You can invite in active meditation while cleaning, cooking, or tending your garden by practicing being present in your emotions within each moment. This mind-body connection invigorates the healing abilities of the body by reducing stress and supporting the healthy flow of life force energy. You can practice active meditation alone or in a group setting. There are many online tutorials and videos that can help you practice at home, or you can attend a class, workshop, or retreat in your area. There is also a wide variety of active meditation music available for download or streaming. As with any type of meditation, it's helpful to set an intention for your session before you begin. You can focus on this intention mentally or announce it out loud as a chant or a mantra (see entries in Chapter 6).

Breathwork

Description

Breathing is central to many movement-based energy healing practices, including qigong, tai chi, and yoga (see entries in this chapter). But breathwork is also a practice in itself. Consciously controlling your breathing can influence your mental, emotional, and physical states, reducing stress and tension and increasing relaxation and focus. Specific techniques include pranayama, Holotropic Breathwork, and integrative breathwork.

History and Lore

Breathwork is an ancient practice that is integral to countless spiritual and healing endeavors. In Hinduism, the breath is considered the source of the life force (*prana*). Pranayama (extension of the life force or breath) is a type of breath control that is incorporated into many spiritual practices. The Czech psychiatrist Stanislav Grof (born 1931) developed Holotropic Breathwork, a trademarked method of accessing "non-ordinary" states of consciousness. Integrative breathwork, described as "an evocative musical journey utilizing breath," was developed by Jacquelyn Small, who founded the Eupsychia Institute in Austin, Texas.

Uses

While breathing is a natural, involuntary process, taking the time to actively focus on the breath can have numerous benefits for both your mind and body. When we're not concentrating on it, we often revert to shallow breathing, which means we don't take in as much oxygen as we could. Consciously taking deeper, fuller breaths can help oxygenate the blood, which in turn helps your body work better, from your brain to your feet. Breathwork is also thought to be a fundamental part of your spiritual ascension, as it allows you to tune into the rhythms and energy of life itself and be fully in the present moment. There are countless ways to use breathwork, from incorporating it into your meditation or yoga routine to practicing it at your desk at work. There are many wonderful breathwork resources available online, but classes and workshops are especially good opportunities to learn from trained breathwork therapists and healers. There are also professional breathwork training programs for those who are interested in becoming practitioners themselves.

Dance

Description

Dance is one of the most beautiful and satisfying modes of expression. From ballet to hip-hop, there is a type of dance for every mood or occasion. In the energy healing realm, dance appears in a variety of practices, usually as a form of tension release or physical expression; an example of this is active meditation (see entry in this chapter). Typically, music and dance go hand in hand, as discussed in Chapter 6.

History and Lore

It is likely that humans have been dancing since our very beginning, but the earliest known documentation of dance is found in 9,000-year-old cave paintings discovered at the Bhimbetka rock shelters in Madhya Pradesh, India. Chinese pottery from the Neolithic period features images of people dancing in lines holding hands. In the ancient Egyptian, Greek, and Roman civilizations, dance was a part of life and was incorporated into many ceremonies and rituals, including funerals.

Uses

Dancing as an energy healing practice isn't very different from dancing by yourself in the privacy of your own home. It is a great way to relax the nervous system and have a little fun, but group classes and workshops offer an opportunity to learn from experienced teachers and to try dances that involve partners or larger groups of people. Many gyms, meditation centers, yoga studios, and other places where you may already have a membership also offer dance classes. You can also incorporate unique forms of dance alongside modalities of energy healing, such as chakra balancing, Reiki, or drum circles. Dance/movement therapy is another option you might be interested in checking out. The American Dance Therapy Association defines dance/movement therapy as "the psychotherapeutic use of movement to further the emotional, cognitive, physical and social integration of the individual." Their website (www.adta .org) has lots of helpful resources and information.

Grounding

Description

Grounding, or earthing, is a practice that aims to reconnect a person to the natural electric charge of the earth. By walking barefoot on grass, sand, or dirt, or by using a grounding mat, it is believed that a beneficial transfer of electrons to the body occurs, thus supporting a variety of health benefits. *Grounding* also can refer to a general mindfulness technique promoting connection and stability.

History and Lore

For Native Americans and Aboriginal Australians, walking barefoot was considered a spiritual practice that connected a person to earth's wisdom. In traditional Chinese medicine, the vital life force energy of the earth, called qi (or chi), was necessary for inner harmony. In India, Ayurveda favored barefoot walks and yoga poses performed directly on the earth so as to balance the soul and body.

Uses

For most of human history, being in contact with the energy of the earth was part of a person's everyday routine. But as grass was replaced with concrete, soft leather shoes gave way to rubbery sneakers, and our homes became further in the sky and less upon the ground, we now need to make a conscious effort to reconnect with the stability of the earth below our feet. Research has shown that grounding can improve sleep, reduce inflammation, and balance cortisol levels. Luckily, grounding is a very simple wellness practice you can do on your own. Simply walking barefoot in the grass, sitting up against a tree at the park, or participating in some outdoor yoga can be an excellent way to receive the healing energy of the earth. If you live in a large city or have other challenges that make accessing appropriate outdoor spaces difficult, you could use a grounding mat inside; these mimic the earth's natural electric charge.

Labyrinth Walking

Description

A labyrinth, also known as a maze, is an intricate structure of interconnected passageways through which it's difficult to find your way. Labyrinths have had many purposes throughout history, from deterring or trapping an enemy to enhancing prayer or devotion. Today, many people enjoy the wellness practice of labyrinth walking, which consists of walking through the passages of a labyrinth as part of spiritual exploration, contemplation, or prayer. The experience simulates the path of life, which is full of twists and turns and where the future is always just out of view.

History and Lore

Labyrinth walking is an ancient practice used by many faiths for contemplation and prayer. The design, while considered a maze, is not meant to confuse. It has been found as far back as 3,000 years in a multitude of cultures such as ancient Crete and the Hopi Native Americans, and in Norway. In Greek mythology, King Minos of Crete commanded the architect and artist Daedalus to design and build a labyrinth to hold the Minotaur, a creature with the head of a bull and the body of a man. The Minotaur was eventually killed by the hero Theseus. As the story goes, the labyrinth was so complex that even its creator had trouble escaping from it.

Labyrinths also appear in the Christian tradition. An example is the labyrinth in the Chartres Cathedral in France, which was constructed in the early thirteenth century. Though little documentation exists, it is believed that labyrinths such as the one in Chartres symbolize the long, arduous path that pilgrims would have followed to visit places of worship during the medieval period. They would be encouraged to walk the labyrinth instead of embarking on a pilgrimage to the Holy Lands.

Uses

Walking a labyrinth is a form of active meditation (discussed earlier in this chapter), and can be a unique spiritual experience. The activity is beneficial for reducing stress, quieting the mind, and increasing self-awareness. Labyrinths are metaphors of life, as they are spaces where you can reflect and receive solutions to what hinders your fullest experience. These spaces support the healthy flow of life force energy; blockages are removed as you gain insight via reflection. The repetitive act of walking a labyrinth also releases negative energy and improves clarity, deepening the connection with the inner self. Setting an intention before your walking session will assist in streamlining energy healing goals. A simple search online will most likely give you some local labyrinths.

Mudras

Description

Mudras are symbolic gestures and movements that are featured in Hinduism and Buddhism, and also appear in classical Indian dance, meditation, yoga, and tantric practice. Although some mudras involve the entire body, most are performed with the hands. In yoga, mudras are often used in combination with pranayama breathwork (see the Breathwork entry in this chapter). The word *mudra* comes from the Sanskrit word *mudra*, meaning "seal, mystery."

History and Lore

During the Vedic period in India (c. 1750–500 B.C.E.), mudras were performed during the chanting of the Vedas, the ancient scriptural texts of Hinduism. When Buddhism emerged in the sixth century B.C.E., the use of mudras was expanded to Buddhist rituals, iconography, and meditation practices. In Indian classical dance, mudras involve hand, arm, and body movements as well as facial expressions. Various Asian martial arts also make use of mudras.

Uses

Mudras can take your spiritual practice to the next level. By performing these gestures and movements, you can enhance the flow of energy, which can benefit the mind, body, and spirit. In the practice of mudras, each finger is associated with an element: little finger: water; ring finger: earth; middle finger: space; index finger: air; and thumb: fire. One well-known mudra you may already be familiar with is the chin (or gyan) mudra, often referred to as "the gesture of knowledge," which is commonly used during seated meditation. While sitting cross-legged or in lotus position, place the hands on the knees palm up and join the tip of the index finger and thumb of each hand. The circle created by the fingers signifies unity and facilitates the flow of energy. There are hundreds of other mudras you can learn about online or by taking classes or workshops in practices such as kundalini yoga (see the Yoga entry in this chapter).

Qigong

Description

Qigong is a Chinese spiritual practice in which physical exercises or movements are performed in a meditative state with the purpose of aligning the body, breath, and mind and and balancing qi (or chi; "life energy"). Qigong is a part of many healing and spiritual practices as well as martial arts training techniques. The term *qigong* comes from the Mandarin *qigong*: *qi*, meaning "air, spirit, energy of life," plus *gong*, meaning "skill."

History and Lore

Qigong is estimated to be more than 4,000 years old, with roots in ancient shamanic rituals consisting of meditative practice and gymnastic exercise. Over time, qigong was adopted into other practices and traditions, such as Chinese medicine, Confucianism, Taoism, and Buddhism. Two important figures in modern qigong are Jiang Weiqiao (1873–1958), who was one of the first qigong experts to introduce the exercises to the public, and Liu Guizhen (1920–1983), who is credited with coining the term *qigong*.

Uses

Qigong is not only an enlightening spiritual practice; it also has numerous health benefits, from stress relief to increasing flexibility and strength. It is thought to cultivate energy and, over time, build stamina. In particular, breathing exercises such as the Buddha's Breath or the Daoist's Breath infuse the body with qi energy, allowing for increased spiritual awareness. With practice, the exercises provide advanced ways to activate your body's energy healing capabilities. To get started, attend a class or workshop so you can receive in-person instruction and guidance from an experienced teacher. If there are no offerings in your area, don't worry; the Internet has plenty of qigong information and tutorials. The National Qigong Association hosts an annual qigong conference, and their website (www.nqa.org) is a terrific source of information about the practice as well as upcoming events across the country.

Ritual Movements

Description

Ritual movements are any movements or gestures that are performed as part of a ritual or ceremony, such as bowing the head or pressing the hands together during prayer. These movements may express a person's intention in performing the ritual, such as atonement, or they may serve as preparation, such as arranging the body in some way for a specific purpose. The word *ritual* comes from the Latin *ritus*, meaning "rite."

History and Lore

Ritual movements are a component of many ancient religious and spiritual practices. A common ritual movement performed in Catholicism is making the sign of the cross with one's hand. The fingertips first touch the forehead, then the lower middle of the chest, then the left shoulder, and finally the right shoulder. In Islam, a series of movements accompanies daily prayers, which are performed five times a day at specific times. These movements include kneeling on a prayer rug and facing the direction of Mecca, the birthplace of the prophet Muhammad. The worshipper bends down to place his head and hands on the floor.

Uses

Ritual movements are included in most religious practices, usually in combination with prayer. If you were raised with or currently practice a religion, chances are you are familiar with several ritual movements already. If not, you may have learned ritual movements through practices such as meditation or energy healing. For example, incense is often used in combination with movements to waft the smoke toward yourself or throughout a space in preparation for meditation or to cleanse a space of negative energy. Whatever ritual movements you choose to try, you will probably find that they add another dimension to your practice, and over time you may feel that they have become a necessary part of your ritual or routine.

Tai Chi

Description

Tai chi is a Chinese martial art that is closely related to qigong (see entry in this chapter) and practiced in various styles, from fast-paced self-defense techniques to slow-paced meditative movements. The term *tai chi* comes from the Mandarin *tài jí quán: tài jí*, meaning "great, ultimate," and *quán*, meaning "boxing."

History and Lore

The origins of tai chi are largely unknown. One legend says that a Taoist monk named Chang San-Feng created tai chi based on the movements of animals. (In fact, some of the movements are named for animals and various natural phenomena—for example, "embrace tiger, return to mountain.") It is more likely, though, that tai chi is rooted in a combination of Chinese philosophy (such as the concepts of chi and yin/yang) and martial arts such as kung fu. Today, the practice of tai chi continues in China and beyond.

Uses

The three main reasons to practice tai chi are health, meditation, and self-defense. Tai chi is an excellent stress reliever that has been shown to ease anxiety and depression, lower blood pressure, and improve the quality of sleep. As a meditative practice, it serves to keep you grounded in your body and in the present moment. Practicing tai chi promotes mindfulness and the ability to tap into qi (or chi), the life force energy. This type of concentration amplifies your body's ability to balance energy and harness self-healing abilities. And while the slower styles of tai chi may not seem very helpful in the realm of self-defense, the movements are the foundations of powerful, fast, and effective martial arts techniques.

Yoga

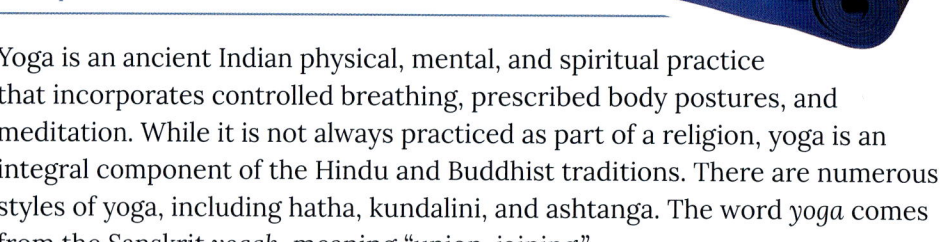

Description

Yoga is an ancient Indian physical, mental, and spiritual practice that incorporates controlled breathing, prescribed body postures, and meditation. While it is not always practiced as part of a religion, yoga is an integral component of the Hindu and Buddhist traditions. There are numerous styles of yoga, including hatha, kundalini, and ashtanga. The word *yoga* comes from the Sanskrit *yogah*, meaning "union, joining."

History and Lore

As a result of the oral transmission and once-secretive nature of yoga's history, it is not known exactly when the practice began. It is generally believed to be at least 5,000 years old, but some estimates suggest its roots may reach as far back as 10,000 years ago. The oldest known written reference to yoga appears in the ancient Hindu body of texts called the Vedas. (Vedic yoga is based on these texts.) According to legend, the Hindu deity Shiva created hatha yoga, a basic form of yoga that has become very popular in the United States. Yoga was brought to the attention of the Western world in the mid-nineteenth century, along with other aspects of Indian philosophy and tradition.

Uses

Regular yoga practice has been found to be particularly effective in combating fatigue and having a positive effect on the nervous system. Certain yoga asanas, or poses, are especially helpful for invigorating the body. For example, Vrikshasana (Tree Pose) helps the distracted mind, while Tadasana (Mountain Pose) supports proper circulation. These asanas target mindset as well, and posturing yourself into specific poses allows for a higher consciousness to channel through you. For instance, Utkatasana (Chair Pose) brings inner strength, while Bhujangasana (Cobra Pose) promotes self-love. These postures are believed to bring you the power to transform your own life through the energy they bring into your system.

Yoga is practiced worldwide, in homes, parks, gyms, studios, and various other venues. There are endless yoga videos available online that you can incorporate into your home practice, but if you're new to yoga, it is best to start with a class taught by a certified yoga instructor. Hatha yoga is a common form that offers all the yoga basics without too many challenging poses, making it great for beginners. Kundalini yoga, which focuses on awakening and channeling energy throughout the body, includes chanting, meditation, and breathing techniques in addition to postures. Ashtanga is a physically demanding style that generates heat in the body, and lots of sweat! This type of yoga is great for those who are more fitness-focused.

10

The Power of Touch

The healing power that touch can provide is unlike any other. The comforting warmth of a hug, the silent understanding of a hand holding your own, and the heartfelt support of an arm draped across your shoulders are more than just sensations; they are messages of validation. In the world of energy healing, touch is an integral part of the holistic approach as it addresses not only the physical body but the overall well-being of a person's mind and soul.

As one of the five senses (along with sight, hearing, smell, and taste), touch is one of the fundamental parts of the human experience. We use touch to relate to one another and to interact with the world around us, and touching or being touched has proven extremely powerful in the realm of health and well-being, both physical and emotional.

Since ancient times, across a multitude of cultures and civilizations, healing touch has been a constant in all forms of energy healing. The underlying belief is that disruptions in the flow of life energy contribute to health issues of the mind, body, and soul. As the understanding of the connection between our energy and physical health continues to evolve, more and more people are finding their way back to the practices of our ancestors, those who incorporated and understood the power of touch.

Each of the practices discussed in this chapter uses touch in a different way. For example, acupressure involves putting physical pressure on specific points of the body with the aim of relieving pain. Massage includes rubbing techniques designed to promote relaxation, increase circulation, and relieve sore muscles. Reiki is a method in which a practitioner places the palms of his or her hands on or near different parts of the patient's body with the intent of transferring healing energy. Along with other topics like acupuncture, reflexology, and even crystal healing, you'll find a variety of options for mindful and restorative contact.

The validation of being touched with a healing intent can allow your body to bring awareness where it may have felt ignored before. The simple acknowledgment of a gentle touch begins an awakening that reminds us we are able to use the life energy we all share in a journey of self-healing.

Acupressure

Description

Acupressure is a traditional Chinese medicine technique that has been adopted by the Western world as a form of alternative medicine. Closely related to massage and acupuncture (see entries in this chapter), acupressure is based on the concept that energy flows through "meridians," or paths, in the body. It is believed that putting physical pressure on certain points, such as the fleshy web between the thumb and index finger, can clear energy blockages in these meridians and thereby restore or maintain health.

History and Lore

In traditional Chinese medicine, it was discovered that pressing particular points on the body relieved not only pain in that area, but also could provide benefits for other parts of the body. Although the Chinese have been practicing acupressure for more than 5,000 years, other countries such as India and Japan have their own ancient versions. This technique was unknown to the Western world until the seventeenth century, when it was first introduced in Europe. It wasn't until the 1970s that the practice took hold in the United States. Today, acupressure has become a popular wellness practice for noninvasive treatment.

Uses

The ancient practice of acupressure has been shown to be enormously effective at relieving pain and discomfort resulting from stress, injury, and chronic conditions such as arthritis, even when other options, such as prescription drugs, have failed. Have you ever found yourself rubbing your temples when you have a headache? That's actually a form of acupressure. Pressing the acupressure point Taiyang, at the slight depression near your temples, for thirty seconds is helpful for migraine, eyestrain, and sinus pain as well. Struggling with motion sickness? Apply gentle pressure at the Neiguan acupressure point (three fingers' widths below the wrist crease on your inner forearm) for thirty seconds to two minutes to relieve some discomfort; this point is effective for treating nausea and anxiety, insomnia, and palpitations.

But acupressure is not just for those seeking to treat a specific ailment. Many people partake in this practice regularly, similar to massage, to increase circulation, release tension, balance and unblock energy, and maintain general health. If you're interested in giving it a try, you have the option of self-treatment or making an appointment with a certified acupressurist.

Acupuncture

Description

Much like acupressure (see entry in this chapter), acupuncture is a traditional Chinese medicine technique that is now used worldwide. Acupuncture targets the same pressure points used in acupressure, but instead of applying physical pressure to those points, fine needles are inserted into the skin. The needles are so tiny that typically you don't even feel them. The word *acupuncture* comes from the Latin *acus*, meaning "needle," and *pungere*, meaning "to prick."

History and Lore

The exact timeline of acupuncture is unknown, but it is believed to have developed out of the practice of acupressure somewhere between 2,000 and 4,000 years ago. Many Americans first learned about acupuncture by reading an article written by the journalist James Reston (1909–1995) that was published in *The New York Times* in July 1971. Reston wrote about his experience of having an appendectomy while visiting China and being treated with acupuncture for the pain following the surgery.

   While traditionally acupuncture was believed to be effective due to its interaction with the body's energy meridians, modern medicine has revealed that the practice stimulates the signaling systems of the body, including the nervous system, which is responsible for the way pain registers in our brains. Like acupressure, acupuncture has proven an effective technique for pain relief in cases where other remedies have been unsuccessful.

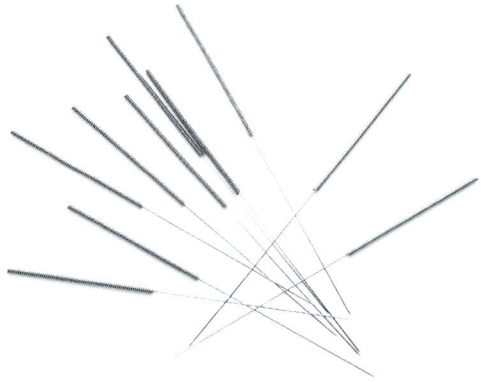

Uses

Acupuncture has gained popularity for its ability to enhance the body's energy naturally. It balances the flow of the life energy called qi (or chi), allowing the systems of your body to work harmoniously. It's also proven helpful for those suffering from insomnia and as a way to improve circulation. It is often used to balance hormones, address burnout, aid in digestion, and encourage mindfulness. Acupuncture is also celebrated for its ability to relieve some chronic pain. Unlike acupressure, this is not something you can experiment with at home. Instead, make an appointment with a certified acupuncturist. They will work with you to customize an acupuncture practice that is personalized to your needs.

Crystal Healing

Description

Crystal healing, or crystal therapy, is a holistic practice and complementary therapy. It harnesses the energetic properties of gemstones and crystals to encourage physical, spiritual, and emotional healing. A crystal healing therapist assesses a client's energy field, and decides which crystals or gemstones will be most helpful for healing. Crystals are then placed on or around the body, and healing energy is channeled and focused. Crystal healing treats the underlying emotional or spiritual cause of a current symptom, rather than treating the symptom itself. The crystals are believed to interact with an individual's energy field to recalibrate and boost the energy field or aura of the person.

History and Lore

The practice of using crystals and gemstones for healing purposes can be traced back to as early as 4000 B.C.E. The ancient Sumerians in Mesopotamia were among the first to record crystals and gemstones as medicinal ingredients. The ancient Egyptians also detail using various stones for medical and spiritual use, including quartz for balancing energies. The ancient Chinese believed that crystals contributed to overall well-being. Ancient Greek beliefs have added much to our contemporary knowledge of healing stones and crystals. The word *crystal* comes from the Greek word *krustallos*, meaning "ice."

The use of crystals as healing stones continued through the Middle Ages, and lapidaries, or books describing qualities and uses of stones and jewels, began to appear. Gemstones and crystals experienced a resurgence of popularity with the birth of the New Age movements of the 1960s and 1970s. Crystal therapy arose at this time as a way to holistically address mental, physical, and spiritual ailments.

Uses

To interact with the energy field, vibration, frequency, and an intentional mindset are required. Since they carry vibrations, crystals are thought to be able to connect with the frequencies in need of altering, thus allowing an avenue to the healing process. As discussed in Chapter 1, different types of crystals have individualized healing properties. Those in need of emotional healing may find rose quartz comforting, while those who are looking for immune system support may choose jasper. Crystal healing is beneficial for stress reduction, recovery from trauma, and spiritual growth. Look for a reputable crystal therapist in your area to start this unique wellness therapy.

Cupping

Description

Cupping, also known as cupping therapy or hijama, is a holistic practice that uses suction cups on the skin for the purpose of increasing blood flow. A vacuum or suction within the cups draws blood away from or to specific points on the body. It is believed to assist with relieving pain and easing the symptoms of certain conditions, such as arthritis, headaches, asthma, and back pain. Cupping may work by the expansion and breaking of capillaries under the skin, allowing for the body to replenish the area with new blood and stimulating healing at a cellular level. It is also thought to release toxins. There are a variety of cupping methods, such as dry (cup is heated to produce vacuum), running (a gentler form of dry cupping where the skin is lubricated prior to treatment and cups can be moved during the session), and bleeding (a needle is used to puncture the skin before placing the cups). The cups can be glass, plastic, or sometimes bamboo or silicone.

History and Lore

Hijama (the word means "drawing out" in Arabic) is a deeply symbolic therapeutic process that can be traced back to as early as 3000 B.C.E. It was associated mainly with Islam and its systematic use arose in ancient Egypt. One of the oldest medical texts humans have discovered, *The Ebers Papyrus*, dated around 1550 B.C.E., describes hijama and details its purposes.

References to hijama cupping therapy have also been found in historical texts of the ancient Greeks. The well-known Greek physician Hippocrates often used cupping as a way to combat disease. The prophet Muhammad promoted the use of hijama cupping therapy, and in traditional Chinese medicine, cupping has been practiced for at least 3,000 years. Hijama cupping resurfaced in the seventeenth and eighteenth centuries along with the rise in public steam baths and saunas. It remained a popular part of therapy and medical practice until the early nineteenth century. Cupping therapy is undergoing a resurgence in relevance today as it's promoted by many energy healing practitioners.

Uses

Cupping can stimulate energy flow, promote blood circulation, and release stagnant qi (or chi), the life force energy. Other benefits of cupping therapy can be to relieve chronic pain, detoxify the body, or reduce inflammation. Many report a feeling of whole-body comfort and relaxation. Cupping is often paired with acupuncture, acupressure, or massage. To find a reputable cupping practitioner near you, visit the International Cupping Therapy Association at www.cuppingtherapy.org.

EFT Tapping

Description

Emotional freedom technique (EFT) tapping is a finger tapping technique used to restore balance in the body's energy field. It is based on the concept of meridian points (energy hot spots), similar to acupuncture (described earlier in this chapter). Instead of needles being inserted at these points, finger tapping is used to apply pressure. It is believed that stimulating these meridian points can reduce stress and dispel negative emotions while restoring your energetic balance.

History and Lore

EFT tapping came about as a result of acupuncture making its way West. In 1962 Felix Mann's book *Acupuncture: The Ancient Chinese Art of Healing* introduced the thousands-year-old concept to a whole new culture. A curious chiropractor named George Goodheart Jr. was the first to try tapping on the meridian points with his fingers. What he noted was how the emotional state of the patient affected the response and strength of the muscles. Tapping began to intersect with holistic medicine when a psychiatrist named John Diamond began using muscle practice, a technique used to assess the body's responses to thought, emotion, and other stimuli, during therapy to rapidly identify core physiological issues. He began using affirmations, or positive statements, while palpating certain meridians to promote emotional healing. It wasn't until the mid-1990s that EFT tapping became what we know today. Gary Craig founded Emotional Freedom Techniques (EFT) by releasing his own tapping techniques as a universal healing modality.

Uses

EFT tapping is a simple process you can try yourself, anytime and anywhere. The practice can bring relief from physical, emotional, or spiritual pain. To begin, pick a main problem to focus on. Give the problem a rating of 1 to 10 in your mind (1 being not much of a problem and 10 being very problematic). Then tap nine specific points along the meridians of your body. (These can be found with a simple Internet search.) In this way, energy is realigned and released to restore balance. Afterward, rate your problem again and repeat as necessary until you feel a significant reduction. Many consider the EFT practice similar to acupuncture without the needles.

Massage

Description

Massage is an ancient form of bodywork that involves rubbing or kneading parts of the body to aid circulation, induce relaxation, or treat pain and injury. Popular types of massage include Swedish massage, deep tissue massage, and hot stone massage. The word *massage* comes from the Arabic *masaha*, meaning "to stroke, anoint."

History and Lore

Evidence suggests that most of the ancient civilizations practiced massage, from the Egyptians to the Chinese. The ancient Greek physician Hippocrates (c. 460–370 B.C.E.), who is often referred to as the father of Western medicine, wrote extensively about massage, stating, "the physician must be experienced in many things, but assuredly also in rubbing." Pehr Henrik Ling (1766–1839), who pioneered the teaching of physical education in Sweden, is often called the father of Swedish massage; however, others claim "Swedish massage" is actually a misnomer and its true creator was Johann Georg Mezger (1838–1909), a Dutch physician who incorporated massage into his practice in the second half of the nineteenth century.

Uses

Massage is both a wonderfully relaxing experience and a tried-and-true method of easing pain and discomfort. It acts as an important routine in spiritual maintenance, as it supports overall energetic health, vitality, and a sense of well-being. There are many self-massage techniques that you can experiment with on your own, but for the full massage experience, make an appointment with a certified massage therapist. Swedish massage, which involves long strokes, circular pressure, and stretching, is what most people in the Western world think of when they think of massage. Deep tissue massage is similar to Swedish massage, but focuses on the deeper layers of muscle tissue, tendons, and connective tissue. In a hot stone massage, a massage therapist uses heated stones to warm and relax the muscles. Due to its potential health benefits, lymphatic drainage massage has become more mainstream in wellness practices. It's a gentle massage focusing on the part of the immune system called the lymphatic system. It is meant to guide lymph, or the water-like fluid that collects and causes swelling in the body, into the bloodstream.

Reflexology

Description

The term *reflexology* has two meanings. It is both the study of the reflexes of the body and how they affect behavior, and a massage technique that involves finger pressure, particularly applied to the hands and feet. The basis of this alternative medicine technique is related to the foundations of acupressure and acupuncture (see entries in this chapter): Practitioners believe certain points on the hands and feet correspond to different areas of the body, and that introducing pressure to those areas can treat ailments and conditions that manifest elsewhere.

History and Lore

Modern reflexology has its roots in various ancient bodywork practices, including acupressure and massage. Though the practice was not documented in any specific way until relatively recently, there is significant evidence that reflexology was practiced by a number of ancient civilizations. In Egypt's Saqqara burial ground, the Tomb of Ankhmahor, also known as the "Physician's Tomb," which dates back to 2330 B.C.E., includes an image that depicts two men having their hands and feet massaged.

Uses

Reflexology is helpful at the physical as well as the spiritual and energetic level. Able to connect with more than seven thousand nerve endings in a single session, this practice is valuable for vital nerve function while combating neuropathy (nerve damage). Many regular users report a relief of stress and insomnia, as well as improved digestive function. Spiritually, it is thought to enhance mental clarity and energetic connection with higher consciousness.

Like other forms of massage, reflexology is something anyone can try, either on their own or with a certified specialist. Resources abound online, from self-treatment techniques to listings of reflexologists in your area. The Reflexology Association of America offers lots of information on its website (www.reflexology-usa.org). The International Institute of Reflexology website (www.reflexology-usa.net) is another great resource, with reflexology charts and a list of trained reflexologists by state.

Reiki

Description

Reiki is a Japanese alternative medicine technique in which a practitioner places the palms of his or her hands on (or above) specific areas of the patient's body as a way of directing energy to the patient for the purposes of healing. Practitioners act as channels for energy, supporting its revitalization in the patient's energy field. The practice is based on the Chinese principle of qi (or chi), the life force energy. The word *Reiki* comes from the Mandarin *língqì*, which is a combination of "numinous spirit" and "energy."

History and Lore

The Japanese Buddhist Mikao Usui (1865–1926) is known as the creator of Reiki. According to the inscription on his memorial stone, erected in 1927, Usui taught Reiki to more than two thousand people during his lifetime. Hawayo Takata (1900–1980), a Japanese American woman born in Hawaii, is credited with introducing Reiki to the Western world. Her teacher, Dr. Chujiro Hayashi (1880–1940), was trained by Usui in the early 1900s.

Uses

Reiki is a noninvasive, complementary therapy that is believed to assist with energetic self-healing. It can support stress reduction, heart health, and sleep quality. Spiritually, it heightens your connection to self and the life force energy we all share. Many practitioners bring their skills to hospitals, hospice care, and group healing circles, as it is a calming and safe therapy for anyone.

A Reiki session is similar to a massage in that the patient lies on a table and spends time both face up and face down so the practitioner can access both sides of the body. Unlike massage, the patient is typically fully clothed. Reiki can be performed in many different spaces such as offices, homes, yoga studios, or even outdoors. Some practitioners can "send" Reiki long distances without having to physically meet. Reiki treats the whole person, including the body, mind, emotions, and spirit. It works on the belief that blockages in the energy field contribute to other health issues, and restoring this natural energetic flow via the hands will improve overall well-being. In addition to the myriad of health benefits, it is also a wonderful relaxation technique. Reiki deepens connection in meditation and creates stronger energetic boundaries for spiritual protection.

The practice of Reiki is available to anyone and can be learned with time and practice. There are many self-treatment methods you can try, or you can visit a certified Reiki practitioner. Visit the International Association of Reiki Professionals website (www.iarp.org) to learn more.

Salt Bath

Description

A salt bath is a therapeutic practice where water-soluble minerals or salts are dissolved in a warm bath while the participant soaks. In addition to relaxing muscles and soothing aches and pains, salt baths are believed to have spiritual benefits of detoxification and cleansing.

History and Lore

The use of salt baths for relieving aches and pains is very common, and widely recommended as a safe way to alleviate discomfort. The practice can be traced back to ancient civilizations. Ancient Egyptians, Greeks, and Romans placed high value on salt not only for its ability to preserve foods but also for its therapeutic properties. Cleopatra was said to have used salt from the Dead Sea in her baths for her daily bathing and beauty rituals. Hippocrates, known as the father of Western medicine, regularly recommended the use of salt water in healing therapies. The popular bathhouses of Rome often included mineral-rich salts intended for healing in their waters. The salt-based chemical compound magnesium sulfate, commonly referred to as Epsom salt, was discovered in seventeenth-century England, and is still used today to treat inflammation, muscle pain, and poor circulation.

Uses

Aside from being a comforting way to unwind, salt baths can bring a myriad of health and wellness benefits. It is thought that the salt draws out the body's toxins through the process of osmosis, aiding in the release of impurities. The potassium, magnesium, and zinc in certain water-soluble minerals can improve skin health, and even offer relief of chronic skin irritations like eczema and psoriasis. Different salts can yield individualized results. Epsom salt, the most popular, is beneficial for muscle soreness, whereas Dead Sea salts are best for skin health. Himalayan salt is packed with more than eighty minerals and elements, making it useful for overall wellness. Spiritually, these salt soaks are meant to cleanse the body and soul of unwanted negative energy, leaving the person clean on a soulful level. Regular salt baths lead to the best results, but soaking for too long or too frequently can dry out your skin. Moisturize and limit your time accordingly.

Glossary

absolute: in aromatherapy, an extract obtained through the use of chemical solvents

adaptogen: a natural substance that helps the body adapt to stress and assists in normalizing bodily processes

aphrodisiac: something, such as an herb or a food, that arouses or intensifies sexual desire

aromatherapy: the use of fragrant materials or substances, such as herbs and essential oils, to affect one's mood and promote overall health and well-being

astral body: a supersensible body that survives the death of the physical body and is capable of ascending or traveling to other realms of consciousness

bodywork: the use of physical therapy techniques, such as massage, for the purpose of enhancing physical and emotional health and well-being

botanist: one who studies or works with plants

chakras: the energy centers of the body, arranged along the spine

chi (or qi): an ancient Chinese principle that represents the life force believed to be present in all things; often referred to in traditional Chinese medicine

counterirritant: a remedy that causes irritation at the surface to relieve a deeper source of irritation

deciduous: a plant or tree that loses its leaves at the end of the growing season

divination: the practice of foretelling future events through supernatural means

evergreen: a plant or tree with leaves that remain green year-round

expectorant: a remedy that facilitates the removal of phlegm or mucus from the respiratory tract

faeries: magical spirit creatures often depicted as young, winged, human-like beings

genera: plural of *genus*

genus: in biology, a category designating a group of species that are closely related and usually exhibit similar characteristics; in a scientific name, the genus is capitalized and italicized

heartwood: the older inner wood of a tree or shrub; it is typically darker and harder than the younger outer wood (called sapwood)

insomnia: a sleep disorder characterized by an inability to fall asleep or remain asleep for an adequate amount of time

lucid dream: a dream in which the dreamer is aware that he or she is dreaming

Mesopotamia: an ancient region of southwestern Asia between the Tigris and Euphrates Rivers in modern-day Iraq; home to numerous early civilizations, including the Babylonians and the Sumerians

misnomer: an error in naming a person or place

Mohs scale: a scale for classifying minerals based on hardness; ranges from 1 (softest) to 10 (hardest)

Neolithic era: the period of human history beginning around 8000 B.C.E. characterized by the development of agriculture

note: in aromatherapy, a distinctive component of a complex flavor or aroma

occult: relating to supernatural or magical influences, powers, or events

onomatopoeia: the use of words that imitate the sounds associated with the actions or objects to which they refer

out-of-body experience: an experience in which the mind/soul/spirit leaves the physical body and views the body from a higher plane or vantage point; often includes travel to other planes or realms such as the astral plane or spirit realm

Paleolithic era: the period of human history that began about 2.4 million years ago and lasted until between 15,000 and 11,500 years ago; also known as the Stone Age due to the early stone tools that have been found dating back to this period

panacea: a remedy for all diseases, evils, or difficulties; a cure-all

papyrus: a paper-like material made of plant pith used by ancient civilizations as a surface for writing and painting

poultice: a soft, moist, heated mass placed on an inflamed or irritated part of the body to stimulate or soothe it

raceme: a stalk of a flowering plant with flowers arranged singly along an unbranched axis; from the Latin *racemus*, meaning "a bunch of grapes"

Raynaud's disease: a circulatory condition caused by insufficient blood supply to the hands and feet; named after the French physician Maurice Raynaud (1834–1881)

reincarnation: the rebirth of the soul (or spirit or consciousness) in another body after death

resin: a substance secreted by a plant or tree that heals wounds and protects the plant or tree against disease

scrying: the practice of gleaning information from images "seen" in a reflective, translucent, or luminescent surface, such as water or a crystal

smoke cleansing: the process of using directed smoke to cleanse a person, object, or area

taxonomy: a system of classifying and naming organisms that indicates natural relationships; the Swedish botanist Carl Linnaeus (1707–1778) is known as the father of modern taxonomy

Index

About the Author

Mystic Michaela (Megan Firester) is a fourth-generation psychic medium. Her true passion is guiding people through Spirit to live their own authentic lives. Michaela currently resides in South Florida, where she has a thriving practice of personal clients. She is also the host of her own podcast, *Know Your Aura with Mystic Michaela*. She has been featured as a New Age expert in *Well+Good*, *Cosmopolitan*, *Shape*, *Women's Health*, *Elle*, and more.